How the Environmental Regulatory System Works

A Business Primer

Aaron Gershonowitz

Second Edition

 Government Institutes, Inc.

Government Institutes, Inc., Rockville, Maryland 20850

ISBN: 0-86587-368-2

Printed in the United States of America.

HOW THE ENVIRONMENTAL REGULATORY SYSTEM WORKS:

A BUSINESS PRIMER

TABLE OF CONTENTS

PREFACE

The purpose of this book is to provide nonlawyers with sufficient background and understanding of the environmental regulatory system to recognize potential environmental problems and to better understand how the legal system is likely to deal with those problems. Such information should reduce costs by permitting better informed decision making and minimizing potential liabilities, and save legal fees by providing information regarding when environmental counsel is needed and what to expect from environmental counsel. The first edition was found to be useful both as background information for business people and as a business school text.

The first two chapters of this book discuss the American legal system in very general terms and should permit the reader to understand the varying consequences of whether a requirement is based on common law principles, a statute or a rule created by some regulatory agency. Understanding the source of the law is essential to determining how that law can be changed and how much flexibility one has with regard to compliance.

The third through sixth chapters discuss the processes by which environmental laws are created and enforced. Special emphasis is given to how regulated parties can participate in and/or influence the creation of laws that may have an impact on their business. In order to make fully informed decisions regarding environmental issues, a regulated party needs a sense of the scope of the powers of the various governmental officers. The discussion of enforcement will therefore include who the potential enforcement officials are, what their respective powers are and the various means by which enforcement actions can be resolved.

Chapter seven provides an analysis of how to determine which laws or regulations apply to your business. The reader should become aware of what types of activities or substances are regulated and how they are regulated. Activities can be regulated in a variety of ways: some activities are prohibited, other activities are permissible only if a permit or license is obtained and other activities are subject to quantity limitations. Regulators, are increasingly using economic incentives as a means of regulation, rather than the more traditional command and control form of regulation. Understanding the means of regulation will help members of the regulated community to plan their activities in a manner that takes all significant risks and likely costs into account.

Chapter eight discusses the impact the environmental regulatory process has had on the interpretation of contracts. By creating liabilities not likely to have been considered when the agreements were entered into, the regulatory process has significantly modified certain contractual rights and responsibilities. In response, members of the regulated community are modifying their agreements. Understanding this process permits parties to make better informed decisions, structure their transactions to avoid some of the potential liabilities one can foresee, and more wisely allocate costs that are foreseeable as well as some that may be unforeseeable.

Chapters nine and ten discuss where to obtain further information on environmental law and the role of environmental professionals. An understanding of both issues can lead to considerable cost savings since there are significant sources of basic information about environmental law that are available without retaining counsel, and wise use of environmental professionals can result in a great reduction in potential liabilities.

Finally, a note of caution may be required. This book is designed as a primer for the regulated community. The general survey nature of the book makes it unlikely that it will provide complete answers to any complex environmental law questions. It should, however, provide the reader with an understanding of environmental law questions, the process by which those questions are resolved and sources of more thorough answers to such questions.

Aaron Gershonowitz
New York, New York

ABOUT THE AUTHOR

Mr. Gershonowitz is an attorney in New York City. His practice centers on environmental counseling, negotiation and litigation. He has represented corporations in the chemical, healthcare, petroleum, waste disposal and waste transport industries, and lending institutions on a broad range of environmental matters including CERCLA, RCRA, TSCA, asbestos in buildings, medical waste and corporate and real estate transactions.

Mr. Gershonowitz has also published numerous articles on environmental topics in publications such as Environmental Management Review, The Practical Real Estate Lawyer, BNA Toxics Law Reporter, Real Estate/Environmental Liability News, Environmental Lab Magazine and Asbestos Issues. He has also lectured on environmental liability and regulatory issues at programs sponsored by Government Institutes, the New York University Real Estate Institute, and The Institute For Health And Human Services.

Mr. Gershonowitz received his law degree from George Washington University where he was a member of the law review editorial board. Prior to concentrating on the practice of environmental law, he engaged in product liability and toxic tort litigation involving products such as Agent Orange and cigarettes. He was also a full-time faculty member at Western New England Law School for several years.

CHAPTER I

WHERE ENVIRONMENTAL LAWS COME FROM

The American legal system is often described as a system of laws and not men. Thus, if your facility is inspected by an environmental enforcement officer and the officer informs you that you need to take certain actions to come into compliance, it is reasonable for you to ask what law or regulation requires that. It is rare that any official will have sufficient discretion to require action simply because he or she believes it ought to be done, and even in such cases, the official ought to be able to direct you to the statute or regulation that gives him or her such discretion. The official ought to be able to give you something that lets you know (1) whether it is the law or this person's interpretation of the law; (2) the origin of that law; (3) the potential penalty for not complying with the request; and (4) the procedure for objecting to the request. Such information is essential to determining whether one needs to comply with a request, whether and how to respond and how one ought to structure future activities to avoid or minimize the impact of this problem. The purpose of this chapter is to familiarize the reader with the possible means by which a law can come into being.

In theory, our government is divided into three branches executive, legislative and judicial and each branch has a different role. The legislative branch makes the laws; the executive branch enforces the laws; and the judicial branch interprets the laws. In practice, however, each branch has the power to make law and does make law. Additionally, all three branches exist in one form or another at the federal, state and local levels. Thus, for each member of the regulated community there are at least nine governmental entities that can make applicable environmental laws. The number is often greater than nine because within the federal executive branch and even within some state and local governments, there are several agencies that can make environmental laws.

Common Law

The oldest source of American law is probably the courts. Our legal system traces its roots back to the development of the common law in England. Common law rules emerge from the decisions made by judges in individual cases. The earliest American common law rules were based on court decisions in which American judges analyzed and built on the early English cases. It is now rare, however, to see any English cases relied upon as authority. Common law rules usually change very slowly as subsequent case decisions modify and refine existing rules or apply those rules to new situations. The principle of "stare decisis" (Latin for to abide by decided cases) generally requires judges to follow existing precedent, and even the most innovative judges regularly contend that their decisions are not innovative, that they merely follow existing doctrine.

Judges make common law rules in three distinct ways:

(1) when faced with a new situation (a case of first impression) they establish a rule for that new situation;

(2) in subsequent similar cases, they refine, expand or limit that rule; and

(3) on rare occasions they create a rule by overruling prior decisions, that is, declaring the existing rule no longer applicable.

The development of the common law rule of *Rylands v. Fletcher* provides a good example of the first two types of judicial law making in the environmental area. In the 1860's, before our collective environmental conscience arose, there were very few limitations on the use a person could make of his property. Indeed, the only two established limitations were the common law rules of nuisance and negligence. One could be sued by neighbors under the law of nuisance if one used property in a manner that is offensive to neighbors and interfered with the neighbors' use and enjoyment of their property. One could be sued under a negligence theory if his or her action caused injury which a reasonably prudent person would have foreseen and avoided.

In *Rylands v. Fletcher*, L.R. 3 H.L. 330 (1868), a mill owner constructed a reservoir on his property which broke through an abandoned mine under the property and the flooded plaintiff's mine. The court noted that this was not a nuisance because it was not offensive use of his property, and that the property owner was not negligent because he did not know about, and had no reason to know about, the abandoned mine. There was thus no established legal theory regarding use of one's property under which the defendant could be held liable.

The court, however, held the defendant liable for the damage, reasoning that the creation of a reservoir was analogous to those cases which had held that keepers of wild animals are strictly liable (liable without regard to fault) for all damage caused when such animals escape. Subsequent court decisions have refined the rule of *Rylands v. Fletcher* to mean that a person who makes an abnormally dangerous use of his property is strictly liable for all damage caused by that use of the property. It is important to note that while the case is viewed as creating new law with regard to use of one's property, the judge still relied on existing case law. The new rule was created by applying an existing rule to a situation to which it had not previously been applied.

As subsequent courts address whether the new rule applies to additional situations, the rule is refined and sometimes expanded. For example, today, courts in many states are being asked to apply the rule of Rylands v. Fletcher to such common activities as the storage of gasoline or fuel oil in underground tanks. Is the storage of gasoline in underground tanks an abnormally dangerous use of one's property so that one would be strictly liable for injury caused by a leak? It depends where you are. Most state court judges that have addressed the issue have said no. In addition to what state you are in, however, the answer could depend on how close you are to a source of drinking water. That is, storage of gasoline underground may not be abnormally dangerous in most locations, but doing so right next to a reservoir might be abnormally dangerous.

Judicial lawmaking by rejecting the existing rule and creating a new one is quite rare for several reasons. First, consistency and predictability are important values in our legal system. Second, because of the first reason, creative judges often characterize their lawmaking as merely choosing which of several existing rules should apply to this case. That is what seems to have happened in *Rylands v. Fletcher*. Third, the law develops slowly, on a case-by-case basis, so that as soon as a rule is stated, exceptions to the rule begin to develop. A judge will thus almost always be in a position in which he or she can be consistent with existing precedent by expanding an exception rather than by creating a new rule.

An example of a court reversing existing authority in the environmental area is the New York Court of Appeals decision in *Boomer v. Atlantic Cement Co.*, 26 N.Y.2d 219 (1970). The Court seems to have concluded that to apply the existing rule would simply be too harsh. Plaintiffs, neighbors of a cement plant, complained of injury to their property by dirt, smoke and vibrations from the cement plant. They sought an injunction against the operation of the plant on the ground that it was a nuisance. (An injunction is a court order prohibiting a party from taking specified actions or requiring a party to take specified actions).

Established doctrine in New York was that a nuisance that is causing substantial damage to neighbors should be enjoined (i.e. stopped). On the other hand, the Court recognized that several hundred jobs were at stake in this plant and the technology to control the emissions did not yet exist, so the question was really whether the cement industry should be permitted to operate. The Court, therefore, overruled the established rule and chose a damages remedy. Some commentators who are critical of the decision have described it as permitting the cement manufacturer to purchase the right to pollute.

Common Law rules are almost always state law. That means that a company doing business in a variety of states may have different common law responsibilities in each such state. Usually, however, because the source of our common law is the same, most states will have the same or very similar rules. In areas in which the law is changing, one can often track a majority rule and a growing trend among recent decisions. The courts of each state are bound by the decisions of the highest court in that state. Decisions from other states may be used to persuade the court which rule to apply, but are never binding precedent. Additionally, a federal court applies the common law rules that would be applied by the highest court in the state in which it sits. Thus, while different common law rules exist from state to state, the location of the activity is likely to govern which common law rules apply to the activity.

LEGISLATION

Legislation Defined

Legislation is what one normally thinks of when speaking about making law. The legislature (it could be Congress, a state legislature or a local body) decides that a rule is needed and writes one. Most environmental law is based on legislation. In some cases this is because of the need for uniform nationwide rules. In other cases it may be because these matters did not become a concern until recently and a legislature can act more quickly and more comprehensively than case-by-case adjudication.

The common law system was not effective in solving many environmental problems. The common law system primarily addresses private wrongs and will usually not recognize a claim when an act injures no one in particular but possibly everyone. In general, one has "standing" to sue (the right to sue) only if they can show that they are injured or are likely to be injured by a particular action in a manner different from the general public. Many environmental issues such as overdevelopment of public lands and protection of endangered species do not create the sort of problems that injure any person in particular. As a result, no one had "standing" to sue and the common law system was helpless to address such issues.

What Legislation Does

In writing statutes, legislatures have an incredible amount of freedom regarding how to proceed. Among their options are outlawing an activity, setting limitations on when, where, or how an activity can be performed, assigning a regulatory agency the task of regulating an activity, or merely providing incentives or disincentives to taking certain actions. In the environmental area, each of the above approaches is used with respect to some environmental problem. It is, thus, difficult to use experience with a regulatory scheme such as water pollution to understand a different regulatory scheme such as hazardous waste.

In addition to freedom regarding how to proceed, our system gives legislatures a great deal of power. For the most part, if the legislature says that's the law, then that's the law. One cannot force Congress to act and one cannot overturn a legislative act on the ground that it is unwise or based on misinformation. The only checks on the legislature are the Constitution and courts' ability to interpret legislation.

Due Process

The chief constitutional checks on legislation are based on the "due process" clause. Due process, in essence, requires basic fairness. Thus, a statute which does not provide notice as to what activity is being regulated will violate due process. Additionally, one can challenge a piece of legislation on the ground that it draws distinctions among regulated and nonregulated activities without any rational basis. The test applied by the court will not be "is the legislation wise or sound?", but "does it have some rational basis?" Courts rarely find legislation to be without any rational basis.

Legislation Can Be As General Or Specific As The Legislature Decides

Legislation can be as broad and general as the National Environmental Policy Act ("NEPA"), in which Congress expressed a policy of the federal government to administer all programs in an environmentally sound fashion (leaving the definition of environmentally sound to each agency), and as narrow in focus as the Medical Waste Tracking Act ("MWTA"), in which Congress was very specific about what wastes must be tracked, who must track them and what the document used for tracking must say. The more general the legislation, the more legal decision making is left to the courts and the federal agencies. Conversely, the more specific the legislation, the less legal decision making is left to the federal agencies. Unfortunately, the specificity of the legislation has no impact on the amount of decision making left to the courts. Sometimes detail gives parties more issues to fight over; sometimes generality leaves more open questions.

How Legislation is Interpreted

Questions of interpretation of legislation are likely to arise in litigation and be left to the courts. For example, the Superfund law provides that owners of property may be held liable for environmental cleanup. The issue of whether a trustee (who has legal title but cannot have personal benefit) is an owner under CERCLA has arisen in a number of enforcement actions. The court's role in such cases is to decide what it thinks the legislature intended.

With regard to interpreting legislation, legislative history and "maxims of interpretation" are helpful, but not decisive. The congressional debates, hearing transcripts and committee reports concerning a proposed law constitute the "legislative history" of the law. Legislative history is often helpful in interpreting a piece of legislation because, when asked what a piece of legislation means, asking what the people who wrote it thought it meant makes some sense. Courts are never, however, bound by legislative history. Thus, when a court explains its view of the law, and its view does not appear to be Congress' view, a court can explain itself by:

(1)   finding the legislative history too unclear to be helpful;

(2)   finding that when a congressional report states an intent that was not specifically written into the statute, the omission must have been intentional; or

(3)   deciding that despite some legislative history to the contrary, the only logical reading of the statute, or sound public policy, requires a different result.

Maxims of interpretation are general rules like "the specific controls the general" or "statutes are to be interpreted as if they were consistent with each other." Such rules are often discussed, but seldom really helpful in interpreting a statute. What most courts do is examine the underlying purpose of the statute and give the statute an interpretation that furthers that purpose. Because that purpose will usually not be explicitly stated in the statute, courts are free to decide what that purpose is and what they believe will further that purpose, and interpret the statute accordingly. Thus, courts have enormous freedom to reshape legislation.

A good example of how courts mold legislation through the interpretive process can be seen in the case of *United States v. Fleet Factors*, 901 F.2d 1550 (11th Cir. 1990). In *Fleet Factors*, the federal government argued that based on the Superfund law, a secured lender should pay for the costs of cleaning up hazardous waste that was disposed of on property owned by the borrower. The court reasoned that the bank's activities with regard to the loan made it the "operator" of the borrower's facility. The court used both legislative history and the maxim that legislation should be read to avoid inconsistency, to conclude that when Congress said that anyone who is "owner and operator" of a facility may be required to pay cleanup costs, it meant to provide liability for anyone who was either an owner or an operator. The court then addressed the secured creditor exemption of the Superfund law which exempts creditors who "without participating in management . . . hold indicia of ownership primarily to protect his security interest." EPA argued that the literal interpretation meant that any participation in management would defeat the exemption. Fleet argued that such a broad interpretation of "participation in management" would render the exemption meaningless because any action to protect the security interest would constitute management (there is a maxim which provides that a court should avoid an interpretation of legislation that renders part of the legislation meaningless or useless). The court resolved the argument by relying on the underlying goal of the Superfund law. It reasoned that the purpose of the law was to require cleanup by private parties. Therefore, any ambiguity about whether a private party was responsible should be resolved in favor of requiring cleanup. The court thus, through interpretation, effectively edited the law to reach the conclusion it thought was correct.

If Congress disagrees with the way legislation is being interpreted, it can always pass new legislation to correct the problem.

Administrative Rules and Regulations

It is rare to see a piece of environmental legislation that does not authorize or compel EPA or some other agency to issue rules or regulations to implement the legislation. The legislative grant of rulemaking authority can be a general statement that EPA may promulgate rules and regulations to implement the legislation or it can specify what EPA should do. For example, under the Clean Water Act, EPA is required to take a number of specific actions such as compiling a list of hazardous substances to which the provisions of the Act will apply.

EPA, like many other federal agencies, performs legislative, executive (law enforcement), and judicial functions. The legislative function of the federal agencies is governed by the Administrative Procedure Act ("APA"). Generally, the APA requires that before a rule is promulgated (i.e. made effective), it must be published in the federal register as a proposal and interested parties and the regulated community must be given an opportunity to comment on the proposal. Most states and many local governments have their own form of administrative procedure act to regulate the creation of regulations.

In addition to the power to create regulations, agencies can create law by interpreting their regulations and setting policies for enforcement. Each piece of legislation that gives the agency rulemaking powers will also define the agency's enforcement authority. There are generally three types of enforcement actions:

(1)   administrative enforcement actions which are decided by administrative law judges ("ALJ") within the agency;

(2)   civil actions in court; and

(3)   criminal actions.

While they normally save the criminal enforcement for the worst offenses, it is not uncommon for the threat of criminal prosecution to be used to coerce a civil settlement. Decisions of an ALJ (judges who work for federal agencies), are a form of agency lawmaking that is judicial rather than legislative. These decisions are reviewable in court, but generally courts give great deference to an agency's interpretation of rules the agency created and the statute the agency is responsible for.

Regulations are like statutes in the sense that a court cannot disregard them simply because it disagrees with them. Courts do, however, have more leeway with regard to regulations than they do with regard to statutes. First, the only check on legislation is the constitution. Regulations, in addition to being constitutional, must also be within the scope of the authority granted by the legislature. Some fairly thoughtful regulatory activity has been overturned as being beyond the agency's power. Second, agency actions can be overturned by a court if a court finds them to be "arbitrary and capricious." While "arbitrary and capricious" sounds like "no rational basis," the standard by which legislation is tested, the two standards are viewed quite differently by courts. The arbitrary and capricious standard gives someone objecting to the rule much more freedom to argue that the facts do not support such a rule. Thus, while courts give a great deal of deference to agency actions, regulated parties have greater success overturning regulations than overturning legislation.

State and Local Law

Most state and local governments have lawmaking powers and procedures that are similar to those described above for the federal government. The key differences are (1) that state and local governments are generally bound by federal law and (2) the procedural safeguards are sometimes reduced. The relationship between federal, state and local law is the subject of the next chapter.

Most states also have regulatory agencies whose rulemaking powers are described in specific pieces of legislation and whose procedures are governed by some sort of administrative procedure law.

It is important to note that even without such a law, there are procedural limitations on what regulators can call the law. At a minimum, for something to be law, it must be written somewhere so that the regulated community can find out what the law is, and there must be some record of the process by which it became law. This rule has its basis in the due process clause of the constitution which has been held to require, as a matter of fairness, that a law provide the regulated community with some notice of what is expected. Thus, when a local health official inspects a facility and says that a number of steps need to be followed to come into compliance, you are never out of line asking the official to show you that rule in their published regulations. On occasion you will find that no such rule exists.

Internal agency procedures and enforcement directives are sometimes a way for agencies to make law without following all the procedures. The agency will distribute to its enforcement staff a directive on what to look for during an inspection and when to issue citations. The directive will often contain material which is not in the statute or regulations but is based on the agency's interpretation of the statute or regulations. Because directives can have an important impact on the regulated community, it is often wise to treat them as law. Such directives, however, are not the law and there are procedural mechanisms to prevent agencies from enforcing rules that have not been officially promulgated or to force agencies to follow proper rulemaking procedures before attempting to enforce a standard.

An enforcement directive is usually designed to address a specific issue. Many agencies also have inspection manuals that describe more generally how to conduct an inspection, what to look for and what to issue citations for. These have the same legal effect as an enforcement directive, i.e., they are not law but it is often wise for the regulated community to treat them as if they were law. Current versions of inspection manuals for many agencies can be purchased through Government Institutes.

The requirement that laws be written and procedures followed does not mean that officials will never have discretion to make certain decisions. That discretion, however, should be found in some written law and is never unlimited. Thus, while we claim that our legal system is run by laws and not men, knowledge of the written law may not be enough to evade regulatory difficulty. There will always be some aspect of the regulatory process that relies on how the regulators are reacting to certain issues. Proving that an official has gone beyond his power can be difficult and costly. Indeed, the costs of litigating the issue may exceed the costs of complying even if one feels that certain requirements have not been validly issued. Contact with the regulators and tracking their activities is thus a necessary part of staying informed about environmental law.

CHAPTER II

RELATIONSHIP BETWEEN FEDERAL, STATE AND LOCAL LAWS

The federal, state and local governments all make environmental laws. As a general matter, when in conflict, federal law supersedes state or local law and state law supersedes local law. On the other hand, there are rules of interpretation that require that laws on the same subject be viewed, wherever possible, as consistent with each other and that in such cases, the more specific law takes precedence over the more general. The ultimate result is a great deal of litigation regarding the relationship between federal and state laws and, unless a federal law explicitly defines its relationship with other laws regarding the same subject, there will be some confusion concerning what law applies. In such cases, it is generally advisable to follow the most stringent applicable law.

Preemption

The ability of federal law to preempt or supersede state and local law is based on two constitutional provisions. First, the "supremacy clause" states that federal law is the "supreme law of the land." Second, the "commerce clause" gives the federal government the exclusive right to control interstate commerce and thus, nullifies state laws that interfere with interstate commerce.

The effect of the supremacy clause can be illustrated by the Supreme Court's decision in *Missouri v. Holland*, 252 U.S. 416 (1920). By treaty, the federal government had agreed to protect certain species of birds that migrate between the United States and Canada. Congress passed the Migratory Bird Treaty Act to implement the treaty and the Department of Agriculture issued regulations to implement the Act. The State of Missouri took the position that the federal government had no right to regulate its birds and sued to prevent enforcement of the federal law. The Court upheld the federal law and the right of the federal government to "override" state law. State law regarding birds covered by the treaty was thus nullified.

The effect of the commerce clause can be illustrated by the Supreme Court's decision in City of *Philadelphia v. New Jersey*, 437 U.S. 617 (1978). New Jersey, in order to protect its landfill resources, passed a law prohibiting the importation of most waste materials. The City of Philadelphia sued to have the law invalidated on the ground that the law discriminates against out-of-state waste. The Court invalidated the law, holding that the Commerce Clause bars states from enacting laws that discriminate against out-of-state commerce.

Finding Intent To Preempt In A Statute

Preemption in its most basic form invalidates state and local laws that conflict with federal law. It can also operate to invalidate state statutes that do not directly conflict with federal statutes. This type of preemption occurs when a federal statute indicates congressional intent that states not be permitted to regulate a particular subject. For example, the Federal Aviation Act gives the Federal Aviation Administration exclusive control over aircraft takeoffs and landings. It thus preempts all local regulation of aircraft takeoff and landings, even if the local requirements do not directly conflict with any federal requirements.

The congressional intent to preempt does not need to be express. It can also be inferred from the breadth and scope of the regulatory scheme. In such cases, courts find that the regulatory scheme is so detailed that it indicates the intent not to leave any area to state or local regulation. Such cases are rare. That is, when there is no direct conflict and no statement in the federal law about the power of the states to regulate the area, courts will usually find the two schemes to be complementary rather than finding an implied intent to preempt. Indeed, in one case, New York State had a program regarding septic tank additives which was so detailed that it discussed specific additives. Suffolk County passed regulations prohibiting the use of certain septic tank additives which were permitted under state law. The trial court found a conflict between the state and local regulations and held that the county regulations were preempted. The Court of Appeals reversed, holding that there was no direct conflict because there was nothing in the state regulatory program to indicate that local regulation could not be more stringent.

There is a trend in the drafting of legislation for Congress to state whether and, if so, the extent to which state or local law is preempted. In the environmental area, state and local laws are often permitted. The unfortunate result is often overlapping sets of regulations from which the regulated community must pick the more stringent aspects of each.

Sometimes, even where there is an express preemption, its scope is limited so that some regulated parties must still comply with both laws. A recent decision regarding OSHA standards illustrates this. The Occupational Safety and Health Act permits OSHA to preempt all state and local law regarding employee protection. California's Proposition 65 applies to all who expose others to hazardous chemicals and is often more stringent than OSHA. The question arose whether an employer in California must obey OSHA standards or the more stringent provisions of Proposition 65 with regard to its employees. A recent court decision concluded that Proposition 65 is not specifically a worker protection provision, so it is not preempted and California employers must obey it in addition to OSHA.

Another approach sometimes taken by Congress is to authorize states to create their own program as long as that program meets certain criteria or is approved by EPA. In such cases, EPA and the state work together to regulate an area. That is the system created by

Congress for such major environmental legislation as the Clean Water Act, the Resource Conservation and Recovery Act and the Clean Air Act. Under such a system, a regulated party will normally have a federal agency or a state agency to contend with, but not both.

Several Agencies Regulating the Same Area

When several different agencies regulate the same area, there is no reason several layers of regulations cannot peacefully coexist. It makes things more difficult for the regulated community because businesses must stay aware of the activities of a group of potential regulators. It is clear, however, that there is no legal impediment to several agencies regulating the same activity. Indeed, there are some regulations that incorporate or refer directly to the regulations of other agencies. For example, under the federal community-right-to-know law, EPA requires that facility operators provide reports concerning all substances for which the OSHA Hazard Communication Standard requires the maintenance of a material safety data sheet. Asbestos is regulated by a variety of agencies, including: EPA under the Clean Air Act, OSHA with regard to employee practices, most states and many local governments. While the overlap can be a regulatory nightmare, there is little question that none of the rules is preempted by another agency.

Having several regulators involved can be particularly difficult when an attempt at enforcement is made. If an enforcement action is brought and several agencies are involved or defendant knows that other agencies are likely to become involved, a defendant must make decisions such as whether to attempt to deal with each agency separately or attempt to address all issues in one proceeding. Additionally, for each set of laws, there are several potential law enforcement officials. If EPA and the state environmental agency are both investigating the same matter, one must be aware that EPA will handle its own administrative enforcement, the United States Attorney's office will handle civil or criminal enforcement and at the state level the same can be said about state agencies and the Attorney

General's office. And, even though the same law is at issue, different enforcement agencies do not always have identical interests. They must be viewed, therefore, as independent actors.

Some agencies work together well. For example, in Nassau County, New York, the local Department of Health often takes the lead in environmental investigations but often does not prosecute violations of its regulations if the State Department of Environmental Conservation is proceeding under its parallel regulations. Consequently, how one reacts to an investigation or investigations that involve several regulators depends to a large extent on who is investigating. There will, however, be little one can do to use the fact that other agencies are proceeding to prevent any agency from proceeding.

Note that while these separate agencies have the power to enforce their own regulation of a given activity, there are limits to the number of times one can be prosecuted for the same thing. A number of procedural doctrines such as due process (essentially a constitutional provision requiring fair procedures), double jeopardy (the prohibition of trying someone more than once for the same crime), and res judicata (common law rule preventing suits on claims that have already been decided) provide a means for the court system to make the same point: it is unfair to prosecute the same person for the same thing more than once.

Relationship Between Courts and Other Lawmakers

While the courts are rarely active in the enforcement of environmental laws, they serve as the ultimate decision-maker concerning such issues as whether the law is being enforced in an appropriate manner and what the law means. Courts get involved when a civil enforcement action is brought, when a member of the regulated community is challenging regulatory action and, more and more when members of the regulated community have a private dispute regarding environmental law.

When an agency brings a civil enforcement action, it is treated by the court as any other litigant. As plaintiff, the agency has the burden of proof and must comply with all discovery requests just as any other litigant. Indeed, discovery against an agency may be easier because the freedom of information act sometimes requires agencies to provide information to the public which private parties would not otherwise be required to provide.

Suits against an agency can be based on the Administrative Procedure Act, based on some other statute or, more commonly, based on a claim that the agency is either failing to properly enforce the law or is enforcing it improperly. Regulated parties have challenged the power of the agency to act, the propriety of specific regulatory action, and even the failure of the agency to act. In such cases, the agency's decision is usually given great deference; courts are not eager to substitute their judgment for the agency's.

When a suit arises between members of the regulated community and someone is alleging that the other injured him by violating some environmental law, the agency with authority for enforcing that law is merely a bystander. Its view of the law, however, can be important. That is, if a question arises as to what the law is or what a regulation means, positions taken by the agency on that issue carry significant weight.

Note, that while noncompliance may be a tortious act, that is, a private party could base a lawsuit on that violation and one may be required to pay damages for the violation, compliance is not a defense in a civil suit. Federal labeling regulations are a good example. In a product liability suit in which plaintiff alleges that the manufacturer failed to provide an adequate warning, the fact that the defendant has followed every aspect of the federal labeling regulations--what to say, how to say it, size of print etc.--will not be a defense. Courts often view such regulations as minimum standards; thus states are permitted to have common law standards that are more strict.

At the beginning of this section we noted that there are cases in which a court may be viewed as an enforcement officer. This occurs when a court needs to enforce its prior decrees. It may, for example, as a result of litigation require a party to take specific action. If the party fails to comply, a contempt order and fines for contempt of court may follow. By imposing fines for failure to take certain actions, the court is enforcing environmental law.

CHAPTER III

HOW LAWS AND REGULATIONS ARE MADE

Legislation

Any member of Congress can introduce legislation, that is, draft a proposed law and have Congress consider it. Upon its introduction, proposed legislation, in the form of a bill, is assigned a number and referred to a committee. Notice of the bill's introduction is published in the Congressional Record. In the Senate, environmental legislation is usually reviewed by the Environment and Public Works Committee. In the House, the Health and Environment Subcommittee of The Energy and Commerce Committee is most involved in environmental matters. It is not unusual, however, to have several committees play a role in the development of a piece of legislation. Thus, Clean Air Act proposals, while clearly environmental in focus, could also be worked on by the House Ways and Means Committee because provisions may have significant financial impacts. Additionally, the Banking Committee may play a key role in proposals regarding environmental liabilities for lenders who acquire property by foreclosure.

A bill can be introduced in either house and similar bills are often moving simultaneously through both houses. Nevertheless, for ease of discussion, the following description of the legislative process will discuss a bill introduced in the House, then sent to the Senate.

After introduction, the bill is referred to a committee, which refers it to the appropriate subcommittee for consideration. At about the same time, copies of the bill are circulated to the departments and agencies that are concerned with the subject matter. The amount of consideration a bill receives depends on how important or controversial the issue is perceived to be. Public hearings may be held as a means for Congress to gather information and further publicize an issue. If a committee decides to hold public hearings, it must publish an announcement in the Congressional Record and it may publish an announcement in other periodicals. Witnesses at such hearings are usually interested parties or experts in the field, and are usually required to file a copy of their proposed testimony with the committee in advance. A reporter is present and a full transcript of the hearing is available. Public hearings provide a mechanism for interested parties to make their concerns clear to the committee. Also, after passage of a bill, these transcripts can provide guidance concerning what Congress intended by the legislation.

After the hearings, subcommittees usually meet in what is called a "mark-up session." A decision is made to report the bill favorably or unfavorably to the full committee, to amend it or to table it. The full committee then discusses the bill and a decision is made to report it favorably to the House with or without amendment, or to table it. Because tabling a bill prevents action on it, it is rare for a committee to report a bill unfavorably.

If a committee votes to report a bill favorably, one of the members is designated to write a report that describes the purpose and scope of the bill and the reasons for recommending approval. Usually, the report includes a section-by-section analysis of the bill. This analysis may later become the primary tool for interpreting the law. Each report must also contain a discussion of the costs that would be incurred in carrying out the bill and whether the bill is likely to have an inflationary impact. Generally, the House will not consider a bill until the members have had three days to consider the report. Committee reports are usually available to the public.

After passage by the House, a bill, now called an act, is engrossed (certified so that an official version is available) and sent to the Senate, where a similar process is followed. The proposal is referred to the committee where there may be public hearings or amendments. The committee may report it favorably to the Senate where again it will be debated and may be amended. If the Senate approves it with amendments, the engrossed House bill and Senate amendments are returned to the House with a request that the House concur with the amendments.

If the amendments are minor or noncontroversial, the House may approve the Senate version. However, if the Senate amendments are substantial or controversial, a member may request a conference with the Senate to resolve the dispute. The Speaker will then appoint the House conferees, usually following the suggestion of the chairman of the committee that reported the bill. If the Senate agrees to the request for a conference, a similar procedure is followed to appoint the Senate conferees. The conferees are only permitted to discuss matters on which the House and Senate disagreed. They usually reach some sort of compromise, but may report the inability to agree back of their house. If they agree, a Conference Report is prepared explaining the decisions reached by the conference committee. The report is not subject to amendment by either house; it must be accepted or rejected.

When both houses agree to the full content of the bill, it is presented to the President for signature. The bill becomes law if the President signs it or does not return it within 10 days with his objections. The President may veto the bill by returning it to the house in which it originated with his objections. A two-thirds vote is required to pass a bill over the President's objections.

The final step in the enactment of a law is publication, the requirement that the law be made known to those who are bound by it. The first publication, in the form of a "slip law," is usually an unbound pamphlet. The heading will indicate the public law number, date of approval, bill number and the citation indicating where it can be found in the United States Statutes at Large (a chronological arrangement of the laws passed by each session of Congress). The slip law will also contain editorial comments by the Office of the Federal Register, including a guide to the legislative history, the date of consideration in each house and where the law will be codified in the United States Code (a codification of the laws of the United States arranged according to subject matter).

The legislative process in most states will be quite similar to the above, but will usually not include such a well documented record of why the legislature took the action it did. At the local level, cities and counties are not likely to have two houses, are not likely to provide as much public notice and opportunity for input, and are therefore able to act more quickly. It is not unusual, for example, for a local ordinance to be introduced and passed at the same council meeting.

As can be seen from the above, the legislative process at the federal level is rarely completed quickly. Prior to submission of a bill and during consideration, a great deal of behind-the-scenes work is done by congressional staffs. However, during the process, virtually all proceedings are open to the public so that interested parties have ample opportunity to follow the actions and make their opinions known.

Agency Regulations

Often a piece of environmental legislation will merely set forth a policy or an objective and EPA will be given the task of drafting regulations to implement that policy or to meet that objective. Thus, regulations that are drafted and adopted by government agencies often have a greater impact on the regulated community than legislation.

The theory behind the extensive use of regulations as opposed to legislation is the need for specialization. Each agency is presumed to have (or be capable of acquiring) greater expertise in a particular subject, making it wise to have the agency set standards and make policy decisions. Both EPA and OSHA possess a great deal of technical expertise and courts often give deference to their technical decisions.

All regulations must be adopted in accordance with some legislative grant of power. Some legislation, such as the Toxic Substances Control Act, contains an extensive list of the types of regulations EPA "may" issue. 15 U.S.C. §2605. Other laws require EPA to publish specific regulations within a set time after passage of the law. The more Congress believes that EPA may not share its view on an issue, the greater the likelihood that Congress will require certain regulations within a fixed time.

The following is an overview of how regulations come into being in the federal scheme. Most states follow similar procedures, but state versions of administrative procedure vary, and may provide fewer procedural safeguards for the regulated community.

The Administrative Procedure Act ("APA"), codified in Title 5 of the United States Code, contains procedures which all agencies must follow in issuing rules or regulations. "Agency" is broadly defined in the APA to include all authorities of the government, with certain exceptions such as Congress, the judiciary and the military. The APA outlines the procedures to be followed by an agency regarding rulemaking, licensing and adjudication.

A "rule" is broadly defined as "an agency statement of general or particular applicability and future effect, designed to implement, interpret or prescribe law or policy or describing the organization, procedure or practice requirements of an agency . . . " While there are times that agency rulemaking and agency adjudication are difficult to distinguish, if the regulated community as a whole or a specific portion of it are involved, it is likely to be rulemaking. If one party or event is at issue, it is likely to be an adjudication.

Not less than 30 days before the effective date of a rule, general notice of proposed rulemaking must be published in the federal register. The notice must contain the terms or substance of the proposed rule, the legal authority under which the rule is proposed and the time, place and nature of any public rulemaking proceeding. There are exceptions to that rule, the most important of which are "interpretive rules" and the agency's power to make a rule effective immediately if it finds "that notice and public procedure thereon are impracticable, unnecessary or contrary to the public interest." "Interpretive rules" are rules in which the agency states its goal to merely interpret the statute and not to make any new law. These do not require public input because they are not binding on the courts.

It is rare that the public interest requires or permits dispensation with the full rulemaking procedures. Such "emergencies" do, however, occur from time to time. Otherwise, rules cannot become effective or enforceable unless the agency follows the appropriate procedures.

After the required notice, agencies must give interested persons an opportunity to participate in the rulemaking process. Participation may be in the form of written statements or oral presentations. It is not unusual for an agency to permit both written comments and oral comments at a public hearing. After considering the public statements, agencies must publish the final rule with a statement of the basis and purpose of the rule. This statement of the basis and purpose of the rule, known as the preamble, is an important source of interpretation of the rule.

In practice, it is not uncommon for EPA and OSHA to solicit input from interested parties prior to making a proposal. The proposed rule will then contain a preamble which contains extensive discussion of the justification for the proposal. Additional comments are then received either at a public hearing or during the public comment period. The preamble to the final rule will usually respond to many of the comments received.

While the above rules appear to be fairly simple and straightforward, a great deal of litigation has analyzed such issues as what actions constitute rulemaking and whether a particular notice was sufficient. A primary means of attacking a body of regulations is to focus on whether the agency did everything right in promulgating them. Most law schools now provide courses in administrative law and administrative law is a specialty in many law firms.

Federal agencies now produce a large volume of regulatory material on a daily basis. Indeed, the daily index to the federal register, the list of actions taken by federal agencies on any day, is usually about 10 pages long.

Negotiated Rulemaking

EPA has, on several occasions, employed a procedure called negotiated rulemaking. In this procedure, the agency invites interested parties and representatives of the regulated community to participate in the drafting of regulations. The primary goal of negotiated rulemaking is to permit the agency to promulgate controversial sets of rules and avoid the protracted legal battles that often follow the issuance of such rules. The rules that result from this process are those upon which the working group can reach a consensus. This process does make rulemaking more efficient and save government time and money, but critics contend that the result of this process is often a watered down version of the rules the agency would otherwise have issued. Because of litigation in the form of legal challenges to the new rule that often follow a rulemaking, EPA is now using negotiated rulemaking more often as a means of both avoiding the costs of litigation and expediting the process.

Hearings

Agencies hold two types of hearings: (1) legislative hearings, where the agency is gathering information and views about a proposal and (2) adjudicatory hearings where a particular issue regarding a particular person is at stake. At a legislative hearing, members of the public voice their opinion about a proposal. An adjudicatory hearing is "trial-like" and adversary. The procedures and rules of evidence, however, are less strict than in most courts. These two general types of hearings permit agencies to make law both legislatively and judicially. The body of agency decisions interpreting the law or regulations can be as important to understanding the law as review of the regulations.

Permits

Permits are, in a sense, regulations that apply to a specific plant, process or individual. Because the Clean Water Act's National Pollution Discharge Elimination System ("NPDES") applies to anyone who discharges wastewater and thus applies to nearly all manufacturers, the permit procedures under this program have a broader impact than most sets of regulations. Additionally, at the state and local level, many activities are regulated through permit systems. The following brief analysis of the Clean Water Act permit system is illustrative of such systems.

Basically, a permit from EPA or the state is required in order to discharge wastewater. States may enforce the Clean Water Act only after they convince EPA that they have the legal authority to implement and enforce its provisions. The NPDES permit will include nationally required effluent limitations and any more stringent water quality limitations based on the water into which the discharge will be made and other compliance provisions regarding such matters as pollution control technology, and monitoring and reporting requirements.

The effluent criteria in a permit are set according to the limits of existing technology. Thus, EPA's view of BAT (best available technology) and BPT (best practicable technology) will play an important role in the process. Since both BAT and BPT require an analysis of costs, the technology-based limitations can be the source of a great deal of disagreement between the agency and a regulated party.

Procedurally, the first step is submission of a permit application that explains the process the applicant plans to engage in, the technology it plans to use and what the discharge is likely to consist of. The application also must contain detailed information about the site, the geology of the site and the water system into which discharge is proposed. This application is then reviewed by the EPA staff or the staff of the relevant state agency. Many agencies have a procedure in place for assistance in preparing the application. This procedure can be helpful in expediting the completion of the permit process. The process for obtaining permit modifications is similar to the application process. A modification will be required for changes in the volume of wastewater, changes in limitations, changes in location or even changes in the owner of the permit.

The agency responds to the application by notifying the applicant that the application is complete or by listing the additional information needed to complete the application and additional conditions that must be included in the permit. Among the standard conditions are:

1. The permittee agrees to comply with all conditions of the permit;

2. The permittee agrees to properly operate and maintain its systems of treatment and control;

3. The permittee agrees to take all reasonable steps to minimize or prevent any discharge in violation of the permit;

4. The permittee may not defend an enforcement action on the ground that it would have been required to halt or reduce plant operations to prevent the violation;

5. The permittee will permit the agency to inspect the facility and review documents;

6. The permittee will agree to follow strict monitoring, record keeping and reporting requirements.

When an applicant is dissatisfied with permit conditions imposed by EPA or a state, it will usually attempt to negotiate more favorable conditions. If the applicant is still dissatisfied, it is entitled to appeal permit provisions. The procedure for review is first an administrative agency evidentiary proceeding, possibly followed by a court proceeding.

An appeal of permit provisions is rare. Typically, once the permit is in final draft form, the public is given notice of the permit and provided an opportunity to comment. A public hearing is required if there is substantial public opposition to the issuance of the permit. Based on this public participation, the draft permit may be modified. If any party is aggrieved, an evidentiary hearing process begins. This is often a full-blown trial with both sides submitting expert testimony concerning why their position is most sound. After a final determination is made on the appropriateness of permit conditions, the permit is in effect.

There is something of a trend in the environmental area to increase the number of activities that are regulated by a permit system. Permit systems provide the regulators with greater information about what the regulated community is doing and permit greater flexibility depending on such factors as the activities a regulated party is engaged in and the location.

When Rules Become Effective

Within the federal register notice regarding a rule, the agency will state an effective date or effective dates. Many rules are effective immediately upon publication. Others, however, require major changes in the way certain businesses operate and, therefore, a phase-in period must be provided. Depending on the situation, final rules may not become effective for two years, or portions may become effective at different times. Additionally, it is not unusual for the final promulgation of a set of regulations to be followed quickly by a lawsuit. If the challenge to the agency's action is substantial, a court may issue a stay of the applicability of a portion of the regulations. In that case, one needs to follow the litigation in order to know what parts are in effect and when the remaining portions become effective.

The General Accounting Office ("GAO") has the power to delay or prevent the applicability of regulations. Pursuant to the paperwork reduction act, regulations are screened by GAO, which examines the costs involved. GAO has, at times, prevented the applicability of certain regulations until either the regulations are revised or further study takes place.

Finally, Congress in requiring the agency to issue regulations can set a deadline for when those regulations must become effective. Congress has, at times, included an enforcement provision, stating that if regulations are not in effect by a certain date, then some other source of law, sometimes an existing guidance document, sometimes state law, will be the means of regulating this area. The purpose is to emphasize the need for the agency to act quickly. An example of such a "hammer" provision is section 112(g) of the Clean Air Act Amendments of 1990 which provides that if EPA fails to issue air toxic's regulations according to schedule, then 18 months after a missed deadline, states must implement such restrictions as part of the permit process.

Executive Orders

Because EPA, OSHA and most of the other federal agencies are within the executive branch of the government, the president can, by executive order, have an impact on the regulatory process. For example, EPA was created by President Nixon's reorganization of the executive agencies. President Nixon took environmental responsibilities from a number of agencies and put them into the new EPA.

The impact of official executive orders is primarily limited to such issues as procedure and structure. The president does, however, also have great substantive impact on the regulatory process. The president's "agenda" for what issues need to be addressed is often translated into both congressional and regulatory action. More importantly, through the political appointment process, the president's priorities often translate into regulatory action or inaction. What rules are being enforced with the most vigor, what regulations are finalized with the most speed and what issues lie dormant, are often controlled by the President. Thus, to a large extent, what the regulated community needs to be most concerned with is determined by the president at the federal level and chief executive at other levels of government.

There have been a number of cases in which the scope of the Presidential power to regulate has been tested. In the *Steel Seizure Case*, President Truman's seizure of the steel industry by an executive order was held to be an improper attempt by the president to legislate. In contrast to that, the Supreme Court has held that Congress cannot maintain a "legislative veto" over executive action. That is, Congress' grant of rulemaking power to a federal agency cannot be conditioned on a vote by one house of Congress approving the regulations. The legislative veto would be "legislation" and requires the full legislative process.

Treaties

The United States Constitution states that treaties entered into by the federal government are the supreme law of the land. Treaties can thus, supersede both state and local laws. There has been a great deal of international activity regarding the environment, especially with regard to issues such as ozone depletion and global warming. Nevertheless, it is very rare for a treaty to have a significant impact on the regulated community.

There are several reasons that treaties have little impact on the regulated community. First, since treaties must be ratified by the Senate, they are rarely ratified if it appears that they impose requirements not already accepted by our political process. Second, an environmental treaty will often bind the President to certain goals as opposed to results. The treaty, as a form of law, impacts the regulatory process by binding the executive to push for certain types of laws or regulations. Those laws or regulations must go through the legislative or rulemaking processes described above. The treaty may be a tool used by the President to assist the passage of legislation, but it is rarely, in reality, either the basis of the legislation or even the source of the goal.

CHAPTER IV

HOW THE REGULATED COMMUNITY CAN AFFECT THE DEVELOPMENT OF REGULATIONS

The regulatory process is designed so that members of the regulated community can have an impact on the development of regulations. Indeed, the system provides numerous opportunities to have an impact on the development of regulations. These opportunities exist prior to the proposal of regulations, after the proposal of regulations and after the regulations are finalized. Some of these opportunities are discussed in chapter III where the rulemaking process is described. The discussion of the rulemaking process in chapter III focused on the acts of the agency. This chapter will discuss how one can have an impact on agency rulemaking activities.

Prior to Proposal

Prior to the proposal of regulations, the regulated community can take a variety of steps to prevent or initiate the regulatory process. The regulatory process does not start on its own. It starts, instead, in response to some problem or perceived problem. It may sound trite to recommend not causing any problems or perceived problems. However, to the extent that an industry polices itself or responds effectively to perceived problems, it can reduce the need or perceived need for regulation. Members of the regulated community must remember that they have two independent duties: (1) compliance with the regulations and (2) avoiding actions that are likely to cause injury. The regulated community gets in trouble when it ignores this second duty or assumes that compliance with the existing regulations is sufficient.

A classic example of this comes from the area of asbestos abatement. In 1986 when OSHA issued very strict worker protection requirements which included negative pressure enclosures, respirators and wetting the asbestos before removal, the regulated community geared up to meet the immense regulatory challenge. The first year, however, one of the greatest causes of serious injury on asbestos projects was electrocution. The regulated community was so focussed on the asbestos that they ignored what happens when water and electricity meet. They soon learned that it is essential to both follow the regulations and keep your eyes open.

Additionally, public education can prevent the perception of problems where no real problems exist. Effective use of or dealing with the press is difficult in this field, but too many regulations exist because the regulated community was unable to convince the public that false rumors spread by the press were false or that concerns raised by the press were too remote to be of great concern. Many firms now use public relations consultants or in-house public relations specialists to deal with such problems.

Causing Regulations To Be Proposed

Since regulations are almost always a response to some problem, the regulated community can bring about new regulation by convincing the regulators that there is a serious problem that needs to be remedied. That is precisely what happened in the fall of 1990 regarding lender liability. The Fleet Factors decision (901 F.2d 1550 (11th Cir. 1990)), sent shockwaves through the banking community. The industry therefore began an organized lobbying effort to have Congress reverse the ruling that made lenders potentially liable for hazardous waste cleanup on a borrower's property. Congress held hearings and, during the hearings, EPA agreed to draft a proposed interpretive rule to remedy the situation. This rulemaking became effective in the Spring of 1992.

It is not always easy for the regulated community to convince the regulators that a problem exists and needs to be responded to. Indeed, the regulators are often less responsive to perceived needs than the legislature is. Nevertheless, lobbying and similar efforts can be aimed at either party.

Another method of bringing about regulation is by litigation. One can bring suit arguing that based on a legislative pronouncement, the agency must regulate a particular substance or activity. It is rare that a court orders regulations, but labor unions have been particularly successful in using this tactic to persuade OSHA to regulate. Additionally, several recent lawsuits have resulted in EPA being ordered to issue regulations required by the 1990 Clean Air Act Amendments in accordance with a schedule fixed by the Court. Often, the litigation raises the issue in enough high places to convince the regulators to act.

From the time a decision is made to draft regulations, until the official proposal, one can still influence the shape of the regulations. During the drafting period, the agencies gather a great deal of information regarding the issue and it is important for the regulated community to get its point of view both to the regulators and to the public. If the public is convinced that regulation is necessary, regardless of whether there is any reason for regulation, there will probably be regulation.

After Proposal

When a proposed regulation is published in the federal register, it will contain a deadline for public comments, a schedule of public hearings (if any), and it will sometimes request additional information from the regulated community. A member of the regulated community should then develop a strategy for responding and providing information if the proposal will have an impact on their business. Because a set of regulations often affects all members of a given industry, trade associations often engage in such activities on behalf of their members.

Contacts with the agency can help guide that strategy. Many in the regulated community react initially to new or proposed regulation that will affect their business by taking the position that we have to eliminate this proposed regulation. Often, however, contacts with the agency will make clear that the regulation is here to stay; the only question is the form of the regulation. In such cases, it is better for regulated parties to spend their resources trying to eliminate or modify the worst parts of the proposal, rather than trying to kill the entire proposal. Agencies are usually more receptive to hearing that certain parts of a proposal must be eliminated or changed rather than hearing that the entire concept is bad.

Expert testimony is helpful in both deciding what comments to make and how to make them. Often, it will be industry's view that portions of the new regulation are not feasible. Experts are needed because the agencies are more impressed by the scientific determination that this cannot be done than the economic or business determination. Additionally, the agency will often provide a summary of the studies it performed or upon which it relied in the preamble to the regulation. Effective comment will study those studies carefully and respond.

Procedural comments are often more persuasive than substantive comments. That is, pointing out that the agency's analysis overlooked something is often better than merely providing counter data or a revised analysis of the same data. The primary reason for that is that after the proposal is finalized, a court will overturn it only if the agency decision is "arbitrary and capricious." Faced with competing analyses of the same data, a court will often defer to the expertise of the agency. Faced with important data not considered by the agency, however, the court may tell the agency to consider this new data.

When deciding whether to provide written or oral testimony, the subject matter of the testimony will play an important role. However, given sufficient resources, there is no reason not to provide both. As to who should appear at the hearing, it depends on the subject of the comments. Many prefer to have scientists address the science and business people address business aspects of a regulation. Others believe that lawyers are best at attacking a proposal or selling a counter proposal.

Sometimes the most important comments merely seek clarification. Agencies are usually responsive to that sort of comment.

While there will be an official end to the comment and hearing period and the docket will officially close, the process is never over until final publication. There are procedures, both formal and informal, for getting additional information to the drafters. However, once the comment period closes, it is best to attempt to provide additional comment only if significant new information can be provided. To attempt to reopen a docket to merely repeat the same points will only get the regulators angry.

After Publication

After final publication, a rule will be overturned by a court only if it is not consistent with the agency's statutory grant of power or if it is arbitrary and capricious. Sometimes, an attack on the power of the agency is really an attack on the agency's interpretation of the statute. EPA's regulation of toxicity under the Clean Water Act is a good example.

EPA has issued regulations under the Clean Water Act to provide limits on particular pollutants in effluent and particular characteristics of effluent. Toxicity is the characteristic of effluent that indicates that marine life exposed to this effluent for specified periods of time is likely to die. Industry groups challenged EPA's power to issue regulations regarding toxicity arguing that EPA has the power to regulate "pollutants," not characteristics of effluent. The court rejected this argument, concluding that "pollutant" is defined in the statute broadly enough to encompass all waste. Thus, effluent is a pollutant, the characteristics of which can be regulated.

Proving that regulations are "arbitrary and capricious" is quite difficult. It requires a court to conclude not just that the regulation is unwise, but that it has absolutely no reasonable basis. When the substance of a rule is challenged as "arbitrary," courts often defer to the expertise of the agency and accept the agency's explanation of the rule. The court's role in such cases has been described as an attempt to answer three questions:

(1)   has the agency adequately explained the reasons for its decision?;

(2)   are there facts in the record that support that decision?; and

(3)   could a reasonable person upon review of those facts reach that conclusion?

On such a standard, most regulations are upheld.

Ordinarily, the challenge to the regulations must be made quickly. However, failure to challenge the regulation should not prevent one defending an enforcement action from arguing that regulations are arbitrary and capricious. Due process requires that regardless of statutes of limitations, one is never required to comply with a requirement that is arbitrary.

CHAPTER V

WHO ARE THE ENVIRONMENTAL REGULATORY AGENCIES?

EPA

Prior to 1970 it would have been difficult to list and describe all the federal agencies that had regulatory responsibilities regarding the environment. President Nixon recognized that this piecemeal development of environmental responsibilities did not properly reflect the interrelatedness of environmental issues. Therefore, in Reorganization Plan No. 3 of 1970, he created the Environmental Protection Agency and transferred to it, functions previously carried out by: (1) The Federal Water Quality Administration which was within the Department of the Interior; (2) the National Air Pollution Control Administration which was within the Department of Health, Education and Welfare ("HEW"); (3) the Bureau of Solid Waste Management which was also in HEW; (4) the Food and Drug Administration with regard to pesticides; (5) the Council on Environmental Quality (formerly an independent advisory agency); (6) the Department of Agriculture regarding pesticide registration; and (7) certain functions regarding radiation criteria and standards which were vested in the Atomic Energy Commission.

By transferring all these functions to one agency, the goal was to create consistency among the federal environmental planners so that in controlling one problem, another was not created, and so that the regulated community would not be forced to deal with numerous "environmental agencies" who did not necessarily share the same goals.

When creating EPA, the President needed to clarify the relationship between this new agency and the Council on Environmental Quality ("CEQ") which had been created earlier that year when Congress passed the National Environmental Policy Act ("NEPA"). CEQ is to act in an advisory capacity, performing research and examining broader concerns. EPA, on the other hand, will be the "operating line organization," setting standards and enforcing standards.

The head of EPA is the Administrator of the Environmental Protection Agency. Directly under her are a group of Assistant Administrators whose positions were also created by the Reorganization Plan of 1970. The powers of the Agency are set out in the individual environmental statutes, and may therefore differ depending on what statute is being enforced. Under most environmental legislation, EPA has the power to issue regulations and enforce those regulations in administrative actions within the Agency, in civil courts and by seeking criminal penalties which can include incarceration. Since the 1988 election, there has been discussion about elevating the Administrator of EPA to cabinet level. President Clinton has endorsed the concept but the legislation that would be required has not yet been passed.

There are ten EPA regional offices and, for most of the regulated community, EPA activity affecting them will emanate from the nearest regional office. Each regional office has investigators, attorneys and specialists whose role it is to enforce the existing standards and assist people with regulatory questions.

The following is a list of EPA's regional offices, the states covered by each office and a phone number that can be used to reach each office:

Region One, Boston:
Conn., Mass., Me., Vt., N.H., R.I.
(617) 565-3715

Region Two, New York City:
N.J., N.Y., P.R., Virgin Islands
(212) 264-2515

Region Three, Philadelphia:
Del., Md., Pa., Va., W. Va., D.C.
(800) 438-2474

Region Four, Atlanta:
Ala., Fla., Ga., Ky., Miss., N.C., S.C., Tenn.
(800) 282-0239 in Ga.
elsewhere (800) 241-1754

Region Five, Chicago:
Ill., Ind., Mich., Minn., Ohio, Wis.
(800) 575-2515 in Ill.
elsewhere (800) 621-8431

Region Six, Dallas:
Ark., La., N.M., Okla., Tex.
(214) 655-2200

Region Seven, Kansas City:
Iowa, Kan., Mo., Neb.
(913) 236-2803

Region Eight, Denver:
Colo., Mont., N.D., S.D., Utah, Wyo.
(800) 759-4372

Region Nine, San Francisco:
Ariz., Calif, Hawaii, Nev.,
Amer. Samoa,
Guam, No. Mariana Islands, Palau,
Micronesia, Marshall Islands
(415) 974-8076

Region Ten, Seattle:
Alaska, Idaho, Ore., Wash
(206) 442-5810

EPA's powers and the means used by EPA to regulate will differ from statute to statute and from issue to issue. For example, with regard to air pollution, discharge limitations will generally not be set by EPA. Instead, those will be found in permits issued by the States. Each state is required by the new Clean Air Act amendments to submit a permit program to EPA by November 15, 1993. With regard to hazardous air pollutants, the restrictions will be technology-based, not numeric. That is, a source will be required to demonstrate the use of maximum achievable control technology. Under the Clean Water Act, as we have already seen, the discharge of waste into a water system requires a permit. Specific effluent limitations and monitoring and reporting requirements will be written into the permit. In this scheme, a great deal of time and effort is often involved in negotiating (or litigating) the terms of the permit, but once the permit is in place, EPA will know whether there is a violation because regular monitoring reports must be submitted. With regard to hazardous waste, the means of storage, transport and disposal are tightly controlled, but there are currently no numeric limits on how much one can dispose of. With regard to asbestos EPA requires that it be notified of certain projects and that certain work practices be followed. EPA is therefore not likely to be involved unless a violation occurs.

More recently, EPA has begun to use economic incentives more often as a means of regulation. The trading systems under the Clean Air Act are good examples. They permit the purchase and sale of allowances (the right to emit a certain quantity of a pollutant) on the open market.

OSHA

Unlike EPA, which receives responsibilities and grants of power from a variety of statutes, OSHA's responsibilities and powers are derived almost exclusively from the Occupational Safety and Health Act of 1970 (the "OSH Act"). The OSH Act applies to virtually all employers, empowers the secretary of labor to promulgate occupational safety and health standards, and provides enforcement powers. These "standards" are the heart of what OSHA does. Indeed, more than 90% of OSHA citations issued allege violations of OSHA standards.

OSHA standards are promulgated in much the same fashion as other rules and regulations, but OSHA has a tendency to take more time in issuing standards and looks more to parties outside the agency for assistance. For example, with regard to a standard to prevent the transmission of bloodborne diseases in the workplace, OSHA published an advance notice of proposed rulemaking ("ANPR") in the Federal Register in late 1987, announcing its plan to regulate the area and seeking information from the regulated community. The OSHA docket regarding this ANPR received hundreds of responses and boxes of information. OSHA needed time to review and digest all this information and thus, did not publish a proposed standard in the Federal Register until May 1989. Public hearings were held in late 1989, and the process stretched over a period of approximately four years.

One reason that OSHA can afford to move more slowly in finalizing standards is that the "general duty" clause permits OSHA to regulate many matters for which it has yet to issue a standard. Section 5(a) of the OSH Act, the general duty clause, requires all employers to provide a place of employment that is "free from recognized hazards that are causing or likely to cause death or serious physical harm" to employees. Thus, when OSHA decides that a particular matter presents a hazard which needs a regulatory response, it can begin the process of drafting a standard and in the interim enforce the general duty clause in areas where a hazard is perceived. OSHA has, on occasion, preceded such enforcement with public announcements or an advisory notice to the regulated community. Once the regulated community is made aware of what OSHA perceives to be a hazard and that OSHA intends to use the general duty clause to issue citations, it as not unfair for OSHA to inspect and enforce almost as if it already had a standard in place.

OSHA uses outside consultants to educate itself more than most other agencies. This reliance on outsiders has subjected it to some criticism and is puzzling in light of the fact that OSHA has, at times, virtually ignored its research wing, NIOSH, in the regulatory process. NIOSH, the National Institute of Occupational Safety and Health, has the role of developing studies and information for OSHA's use in developing standards. It performs research and makes recommendations to OSHA. NIOSH has prepared research documents on numerous issues and substances. OSHA standards on some of these issues and substances are based in part on NIOSH research.

The OSH Act gives OSHA the power to issue standards that preempt state standards unless the state is operating a program approved by OSHA. Some 20 jurisdictions now operate their own OSHA program. They are: Alaska, Arizona, Hawaii, Indiana, Iowa, Kentucky, Maryland, Michigan, Minnesota, Nevada, New Mexico, North Carolina, Oregon, Puerto Rico, South Carolina, Tennessee, Utah, Vermont, Virgin Islands, Virginia, Washington and Wyoming. Some additional states operate OSHA programs for their state and local employees (state and local governments are exempt from federal OSHA requirements). In other states, the state government has no role in employee health and safety.

OSHA has issued standards relating to particular industries, activities and substances. The substance-specific standards, the air contaminants standard and the hazard communication standard probably have the greatest environmental impact. Substance-specific standards regulate employee exposure to and handling of particular hazardous substances such as asbestos and benzene. The air contaminants standard regulates employee exposure to nearly 300 air contaminants. For each air contaminant, OSHA sets a PEL (permissible exposure limit) and an approved testing methodology. The Hazard Communication standard requires all employers to provide employees with information and training regarding hazardous substances in the workplace. While the goal of these standards is worker protection, they protect the environment in two ways: (1) environmental exposure is limited by the limits on worker exposure; and (2) it raises consciousness regarding the presence and effects of hazardous chemicals.

OSHA has authority to inspect workplaces and impose penalties for violations. Until very recently, the maximum penalty for a willful or repeated violation of an OSHA standard was $10,000, much less than for violation of most other environmental laws. The Omnibus Budget Reconciliation Act of 1990 increased the maximum penalty to $70,000. Prior to the increase, OSHA did issue some very large penalties, but to do so, it had to find hundreds of violations.

Other Federal Agencies

EPA and OSHA are the primary federal environmental regulators. They are not, however, the only ones. Other agencies may have regulatory programs with regard to specialized areas that affect the environment. For example, each of the following agencies has regulatory powers with regard to wetlands: the Army Corps of Engineers, the Fish and Wildlife Service, EPA and the Agriculture Department's Soil Conservation Service.

State and Local Agencies

Most states have agencies whose primary role is environmental protection. These agencies work with EPA on a variety of issues and one must closely examine the relevant regulatory scheme to determine which agency will be most involved. For example, in the medical waste area, EPA and states coordinate their activities and federal law permits state enforcement only if the state regulations are at least as stringent as EPA. In the clean water area, the pollution discharge elimination system has been delegated to many states so that while EPA regulations will apply, the discharge permit is negotiated with the state agency instead of EPA. On other issues, the coordination between agencies is more informal and can only be determined by contacts with the agencies.

In many states, a department of health will have some environmentally related authority. The relationship between the health department and the environmental agency should be defined in the statutes that empower each agency. There may, however, be some overlap.

At the local level, there may be departments whose primary jurisdiction is the environment, as well as health and sanitation departments that may have additional environmental responsibilities. Each of these agencies should have responsibilities that are defined by legislation and may have the power to regulate activities that are already regulated by EPA or the state. There may also be local planning boards whose role may involve land use planning which can have importance regarding environmental issues. The federal community right-to-know law requires that local emergency planning committees be given certain information about the use and storage of hazardous chemicals.

It is often not an easy task to compile a list of all agencies that have regulations relevant to a particular facility or activity. That task, however, should be step one in preparing a compliance program. It often takes some detective work and numerous phone calls, but the time spent can be worthwhile because being unaware of the law is virtually never a defense to environmental violations.

Criminal Prosecutors

At the federal, state and local levels, criminal sanctions exist for many environmental violations. While most agencies only institute criminal prosecutions for environmental violations that are particularly egregious, that is a matter of practice and not necessarily the law. Under many statutes, criminal proceedings can be and have been instituted for environmental violations that are not alleged to be intentional and are not alleged to have caused any injury. One reason that an agency may opt for criminal prosecution rather than civil in such cases is that some environmental agencies are so understaffed and overworked that some of their caseload gets shifted to the criminal prosecutor for reasons unrelated to the violation.

At the federal level, criminal enforcement is by the U.S. Attorney's office which is within the Department of Justice. At the state level, criminal enforcement is usually by the State Attorney General's office. At the local level, District Attorneys prosecute environmental crimes. In many states, local district attorneys have power to enforce state laws as well.

There are often no set rules concerning the relationship between the regulatory agency and the enforcement officials. One thing that is clear, however, is that these law enforcement officials do not derive their powers from the agency. Thus, it is possible for the agency and the law enforcement officers to disagree on whether a prosecution is necessary or on the scope of a prosecution and the law enforcement officials are not bound by the agency's view.

In sum, the number of environmental regulatory agencies that can be involved in any one action is large and growing.

CHAPTER VI

HOW ENVIRONMENTAL LAWS ARE ENFORCED

Each piece of environmental legislation specifies the government's enforcement powers. Those powers can differ significantly from statute to statute. For example, section 309 of the Clean Water Act gives EPA the power to issue compliance orders, to commence civil actions, to seek a variety of criminal penalties, including imprisonment for intentional violations, and provides for administrative penalties, a procedure for enforcing them and judicial review. Many environmental statutes do not empower EPA to issue compliance orders without some prior proceeding. Additionally, until the 1990 Amendments, the Clean Air Act did not empower EPA to seek criminal penalties. While differences will exist from statute to statute, there are some fairly broad generalizations we can make about how EPA enforces its laws and regulations.

How EPA Discovers Violations

EPA can become aware of a violation in one of three ways: (1) EPA has the power to perform inspections of facilities pursuant to a number of statutes including RCRA and TSCA; (2) A number of statutes contain notice and reporting requirements that require parties to notify EPA regarding certain activities, to report certain releases or to report test results. Such self reporting sometimes informs EPA of a violation or of an activity which the agency may investigate; (3) Perhaps the most common way for EPA to become aware of a violation is for someone, often an employee of the facility owner or operator, to call the agency and report a violation. EPA operates a number of hotlines that facilitate this reporting.

EPA has fairly broad authority to inspect facilities and documents. As with enforcement powers, the inspection powers and procedures differ from statute to statute. For example, under TSCA, EPA inspections can be made only upon prior written notice to the party to be inspected. Other statutes only limit the authority to investigate to reasonable times, generally meaning during regular business hours, unless some special circumstances exist. A member of the regulated community may refuse to permit the inspection, in which case, if EPA wishes to inspect, it must obtain a warrant, a court order permitting the inspection. In the alternative, if EPA anticipates a serious problem, it may obtain a warrant in advance. It is not common for regulated parties to require a regulatory agency to obtain warrant. Many regulated parties fear that requiring a warrant will result in a stricter inspection and, if violations are found, a harsher penalty.

The inspection can include a review of documents, facilities and activities. EPA will have a good sense of what to look for and what sort of regulated activities are performed at a facility by knowing what business the facility is in. EPA will know the general scope of a facility's activities prior to the inspection and may gather other information about the facility, the owner or the operator prior to the inspection. Often, the inspector will take samples or pictures which will be analyzed by EPA following the inspection. Thus, the fact that the inspector may leave without issuing any citations does not necessarily mean that no citation will be issued.

If EPA hears about a violation from an employee or other person, it will not usually issue citations based solely on such information. It may write to request information regarding a particular incident or activity, or it may perform an inspection. EPA does not have a large investigative staff, but is does investigate problems it is made aware of.

EPA'S Enforcement Options

Generally, EPA can respond to a perceived violation in one of five ways. First, it can issue a warning letter. These letters describe the alleged violation, the action that must be taken to remedy it and usually contain a deadline by which the regulated party must come into compliance or face an enforcement action. These letters also provide an opportunity to discuss the situation with the agency.

Second, EPA may issue an administrative order requiring that a certain activity be ceased, requiring compliance by a specified dated, or requiring certain tests to be performed. If you receive such an order, you generally have a right to respond by citing defenses or objections, and a right to confer with EPA regarding such orders. Such orders are enforceable in civil actions. EPA's power to issue orders that are enforceable in court is extremely limited and one must examine the specific statutory authority closely.

Third, EPA may take action with regard to the regulated party's permit. Among EPA's options are to seek to revoke or modify an existing permit, or to seek to add conditions to permits that are being negotiated or renewed. Any action EPA can take regarding failure to comply with the statute, it can also take regarding failure to comply with permit requirements (warning letter, civil enforcement, etc.). Attempting to revoke a permit can be a drastic remedy because many facilities would be closed down by revocation of the discharge or other permit. Agencies have, at times, included nonpermit issues in permit renewal negotiations. Thus, even if an alleged violation is not permit related, an agency can take permit related action in response to it.

Fourth, EPA can initiate a civil enforcement action. The relief sought by EPA may be injunctive seeking an order prohibiting a certain activity or requiring a certain action or EPA may seek monetary relief in the form of civil penalties. EPA's civil enforcement power usually includes the power to proceed in an administrative or judicial forum. The maximum amount of money EPA can receive as a civil penalty is listed in each statute and varies among the statutes. That maximum is usually stated in terms of per violation per day. EPA also has policies in place to assist in determining the appropriate penalty.

Fifth, EPA can request that the Justice Department initiate criminal proceedings. In such cases, just like 4any other criminal proceeding, the government must prove its case beyond a reasonable doubt. Criminal sanctions can include incarceration, but except in the most egregious cases, are usually in the form of criminal fines. These fines are not usually any larger than civil fines that may be imposed for similar actions. What makes criminal sanctions more onerous is the stigma attached. Because of that stigma, it is not unusual for a regulated party to "settle" a criminal proceeding by entering a civil consent order that includes payment of a civil penalty and dismissal of the criminal charges.

While there is no set rule as to which type of enforcement action will be taken, a number of the factors considered are: (1) the seriousness of the violation; (2) the intent to violate; (3) a history of noncompliance; and (4) the perceived need for a deterrent effect in the community at large. Thus, it is rare to see a criminal proceeding in which the government is not alleging that the violation was intentional or reckless, and first time paperwork violations are usually dealt with administratively rather than in court. Additionally, failure to comply with very new regulations often results in a warning letter, unless the violation is perceived to be significant or intentional.

Regardless of the enforcement option chosen, there will be procedures to object to the government's position and make your position heard. As a general matter, penalties cannot be imposed until the regulated party receives notice of the alleged violation and has an opportunity to state its position. The first step often recommended in planning a defense is to perform an investigation into the incident. Unless the regulated party has a clear picture of what happened, it cannot begin to consider how to respond. Relevant documents should be reviewed and interviews of the persons who were most involved should be performed. At the same time, the regulated party should find out what the agency knows. This can be done informally, by discovery requests or by Freedom of Information Act requests.

Regardless of what means EPA chooses to pursue enforcement, it makes little sense to simply ignore them. Stay in touch with the agency even if only to request additional time. It is fairly rare for there to be serious factual disputes over issues such as whether there was a release or what substance is involved. Thus, it is more common to resolve these by negotiating terms of compliance or timing or penalties. Most enforcement actions are resolved by the entry of a consent agreement.

If there is litigation, the procedural rules of the forum chosen by the government will control. The action will be treated virtually the same as any other piece of civil litigation. The government will have the burden of proving its case by a preponderance of the evidence (i.e., it must prove it is more likely than not that the accused committed the violation). As with any other piece of litigation, it can be quite costly and it can take years to resolve.

It is quite unusual for the government to proceed against someone in a civil action and a criminal action simultaneously. There is, however, no legal impediment to such a procedure. The theory that supports this "double" prosecution is that the two actions have different goals. The goal of a civil action is compensation or remediation. The goal of a criminal action is punishment.

OSHA Enforcement

OSHA's inspection powers are similar to those of EPA. It performs "programmed" inspections pursuant to an established plan to inspect a given industry and "unprogrammed" inspections in response to a particular suspected violation. The OSH Act provides a schedule of penalties for willful, serious, nonserious and failure to abate violations. Until 1990, the maximum penalty for a willful violation was $10,000, much less than the maximum penalties EPA could oppose. The Omnibus Budget Reconciliation Act of 1990 increased the maximum penalty sevenfold.

A citation will usually include a proposed penalty, but through negotiation one can usually resolve a citation for considerably less than the proposed penalty. To contest the citation, you need to send a letter of contest within 15 working days after issuance of the citation. Failure to contest within the time period is binding. Thus, you should always respond quickly to an OSHA citation.

OSHA citations are contested before the Occupational Safety and Health Review Commission ("OSAHRC"). OSAHRC is an independent agency, not related to OSHA. The judges are Administrative Law Judges and procedures are somewhat flexible. Pre-trial discovery is permitted and OSHA has the burden of proving the violation. Appeal from OSAHRC decisions is directly to federal courts of appeal.

Private Enforcement

Private enforcement can take the form of an action by a purchaser of property against the seller arising out of contamination, or suits by environmental groups acting in the public interest. Groups such as the Natural Resource Defense Council ("NRDC") are very active in attempting to assure compliance with environmental laws as well as in using the courts to broaden the law and increase compliance requirements. They litigate extensively, both against private parties who they perceive to be violating the law and EPA regarding the promulgation and enforcement of regulations.

Both types of suits play an important role in the development of environmental law and can have an impact on agency actions. For example, private cost recovery actions under the superfund law can help further define the PRP concept and thus either expand or limit the parties EPA can pursue for superfund cleanup. In chapter II we discussed how the "standing" issue played a key role in preventing the private legal system from remedying many environmental problems. Private actions are now more common because: (1) some statutes explicitly grant private individuals standing to sue to enforce provisions of the statute and (2) the statutory expansion of environmental rights has increased the number of people who have standing to sue with regard to a particular event.

Some states, such as California, not only permit suits by private citizens to enforce environmental laws, they encourage them. For example, California's Proposition 65, an environmental law passed by referendum rather than by the legislature, contains a "bounty hunter" provision which permits private individuals to bring enforcement suits and collect a portion of the fine imposed by the court. A number of states are now considering similar provisions since such provisions may accomplish the goal of greater environmental enforcement without the commensurate increase in state expenditures.

Public Involvement In Permitting

Another sort of citizen enforcement is based on the right of the public to participate in certain permitting activities. Both the Clean Air and Clean Water Acts provide pubic notice requirements and contain provisions regarding public hearings and when members of the public may challenge permit provisions.

Additionally, NEPA and numerous similar state laws require governmental agencies to prepare or require the preparation of an environmental impact statement ("EIS") before approving certain projects. Permits or zoning changes are examples of such approvals. The EIS is a study of the potential impacts of the project with an explanation of how those impacts are going to be minimized. These statutes usually provide for public notice and the opportunity to comment. Citizens groups often use that opportunity to comment effectively. They may also bring groups of local residents to a public hearing to oppose a project.

In addition to this "political" pressure citizens groups can assert to stop a project, these groups also use litigation as a means of preventing or delaying a project. These statutes require that a hard look be taken at all the possible impacts. It is thus, not difficult for groups to find some possible impact that may not have been properly considered. There has been a great deal of litigation regarding what impacts must be considered. Some significant examples are the developing law regarding what other proposed projects need to be considered, and a recent decision that the psychological impact on neighbors of nuclear power plants need not be considered.

CHAPTER VII

WHAT REGULATIONS APPLY TO WHAT BUSINESS ACTIVITIES

To determine what regulations apply to your business, start with an examination of the activities you engage in and the substances handled. This chapter will attempt to give the reader an idea of the scope of the types of activities covered by environmental laws. It would be impossible to list all of the businesses or activities that are covered. This chapter, however, includes numerous examples of activities that may cause a business to be covered. Because most environmental regulations address specific activities or substances, but not specified businesses, the covered activities of the members of an industry may vary.

PURCHASE OR SALE OF REAL PROPERTY

Superfund

Every purchase or sale of real property is affected, to some extent, by the Superfund law. The law provides that if there is a release of a hazardous substance from a facility, the owner or operator of the facility and any person who owned or operated the facility at the time the hazardous substance was disposed of or released are potentially responsible for all costs of response or cleanup and for any damage to natural resources caused by the release. Thus, every purchaser becomes potentially responsible for cleanup upon becoming owner of the property.

Under the Superfund law, the federal government is required to create a national priorities list of hazardous waste sites. Sites on the list are given priority in government- required cleanups. The Superfund law permits the government to clean up a site and then require the potentially responsible parties to pay or to simply bring a suit to require the potentially responsible parties to clean up the site.

The Superfund law includes a private right of action by those who are injured by the release of a hazardous substance. This includes those who incur response or remedial costs (i.e. those who cleanup their own property). Thus, a purchaser of real property who discovers contamination and cleans it up may be entitled to sue the prior owner or the person responsible for disposing of waste on the property under the Superfund law and require them to pay both the costs of investigation and the costs of cleanup. These suits can become quite complex because each prior owner and tenant is potentially responsible. It is clear, however, that the Superfund law provides both a serious potential liability for purchasers and a means of shifting that liability to the seller.

Largely because of Superfund, most sales of commercial real property include some sort of environmental assessment. An environmental assessment is a review of the property for potential sources of contamination. Generally, an environmental consultant examines the property and as much documentation concerning the property as is available to determine what prior uses of the property or of neighboring property may be a source of contamination. Among the documents reviewed are land registry records and government files relating to environmental compliance. The consultant then examines the property visually, for signs of potential contamination. A report is then written which should explain in detail what the consultant examined and what he saw. The report may also contain suggestions for remedial action or for further testing.

The assessment described above is commonly called Phase I. Phase II additional testing is not commonly performed unless Phase I uncovered some reason to perform additional testing.

The assessment serves two purposes. First, it helps inform the purchaser regarding the value of the property. Property which is contaminated will cost less than uncontaminated property. Second, the Superfund law provides a defense for innocent property owners--those who purchased without awareness of contamination and took all necessary reasonable steps to discovery the contamination prior to purchase. While the law is unclear as to what level of inquiry will satisfy this requirement, at a minimum, the phase I assessment described above should be performed. Phase II of the assessment would include soil and groundwater samples and is usually performed only if there is something in phase I that indicates the need. A consultant or environmental counsel can provide advice regarding whether additional inquiry is necessary or likely to be helpful.

Contracting For Sales

In addition to an environmental assessment, a purchaser can, by contract, protect himself from some of the consequences of environmental contamination. Chief among these contractual means of protection is the environmental indemnity. An indemnity is an agreement to protect someone from certain costs or claims that may be asserted against them. An insurance policy is an indemnity agreement. In an environmental indemnity, the seller typically agrees to indemnify the buyer for costs the buyer may incur as a result of the presence of hazardous substances on the property. This indemnity may be limited to certain substances, to a specific time period or to costs not to exceed a certain amount. It is a matter of the buyer and seller agreeing to how they want to allocate costs of known contamination or the uncertainty of whether there is contamination.

It is not unusual to both perform an assessment and allocate this risk by contract. The auditing process is not perfect. It is virtually impossible to assure that there is no contamination. Thus, one does an assessment to minimize the possibility that there is unknown contamination and then by contract allocates the risk that there may be unknown contamination.

Asbestos

The assessment of a building should contain some discussion of asbestos. Asbestos is a hazardous substance that was used extensively for insulation, fireproofing and a variety of other building materials. Most buildings built between the end of World War II and 1970 contain some asbestos-containing building materials.

There are numerous federal, state and local laws and regulations relating to the proper handling of asbestos and worker exposure to asbestos. At the federal level the chief programs are: (1) EPA's NESHAPS (National Emission Standards for Hazardous Air Pollutants) program which prohibits renovation and demolition projects that will affect certain quantities of asbestos unless EPA is notified and specific work practices are followed; (2) OSHA's asbestos standards that set a permissible exposure limit, and provide specific work practices, handling techniques and protective measures for people who work with asbestos; and (3) AHERA (the Asbestos Hazard Emergency Response Act or the asbestos in schools program), which requires schools to inspect for asbestos and create a management plan that outlines the response actions to be taken. Many states and localities also have asbestos laws, many of which regulate the training and certification of asbestos workers and inspectors. This mass of regulations has made handling asbestos very expensive and has thus made it important for building purchasers to obtain asbestos-related information.

The purchase or sale of a building does not necessarily give rise to any requirements under these laws because the requirements apply primarily to those who work with asbestos or disturb it. Additionally, the presence of asbestos in a building is not necessarily a health hazard; it becomes a hazard when fibers are released to the air, usually as a result of some disturbance. Nevertheless, it is wise at the time of sale, to consider the potential costs related to the presence of asbestos and allocate them in the contract because one cannot be sure that they will never, by renovation or otherwise, disturb the asbestos.

ECRA Laws

New Jersey's Environmental Cleanup Response Act (commonly known as ECRA, but amended and renamed by legislation passed in June 1993, the Industrial Site Recovery Act) imposes restrictions on the transfer of real property and the cessation of certain business operations. Basically, prior to transfer of ownership or cessation of business operations, ECRA requires an environmental audit and cleanup. The specifics of the type of audit and cleanup are subject both to detailed regulations and some discretion by New Jersey's Department of Environmental Protection. The law has added much time and expense to real estate transactions in New Jersey. A number of other states have passed ECRA-type laws. Thus, prior to engaging in a transaction one should determine whether the state in which the property is located has such a law.

Lending and Taking a Security Interest In Real Property

The considerations relevant to lenders are quite similar to the considerations relevant to the purchase and sale of real property. Lenders face potential Superfund liabilities when they foreclose or participate in management decisions in order to protect their security interest. What level of participation in management will make a lender into an "owner" or "operator" of the facility for Superfund purposes is a controversial question. The leading case, *United States v. Fleet Factors Corp.*, 901 F.2d 1550 (11th Cir. 1990) held that a lender could be liable if its participation in management indicates that it had the ability to influence hazardous waste decisions. Other courts have required participation in day-to-day management, a position favored by the lending industry. It is interesting to note that the Superfund law contains an exclusion from the definition of owner or operator which, on its face, appears to be intended to protect lenders. It provides that one is not an owner or operator if they hold "indicia of ownership" solely to protect a security interest. This provision has not served to shield lenders from liability.

In April of 1992, EPA published a regulation interpreting this provision and attempting to create a safe harbor for lenders. The rule should resolve some of the questions left open by Fleet Factors, but does not address all of a lender's concerns. Thus, prudent lenders will continue to engage in due diligence as a means of protection from environmental concerns.

Lenders also need to be concerned with potential sources of contamination on the property and the facility owner's environmental compliance record because these may impact the value of their security or the ability of the borrower to repay the loan. The value of the security would be impaired by contamination because if the bank were to foreclose, it may be unable to sell the property without remediation. Thus contamination effectively reduces the value of the property. The ability of the borrower to repay the loan could be impacted by the borrower's need to take expensive remedial action.

CONSTRUCTION

Environmental Review Laws

New construction is subject to regulation pursuant to state and federal laws that require an environmental review before agencies approve projects. Since state and local approval of construction projects is more common than federal, the states play a greater role in this area. The environmental review could be limited to the submission of a form that explains that there will be no significant environmental impacts, or it could include preparation of an Environmental Impact Statement that involves months of study and is several hundred pages long. It depends on the project.

While these environmental review laws are primarily viewed as affecting development of previously undeveloped land, their impact is much broader. The most common use of these review laws is with regard to issues such as whether to permit commercial development of a piece of land and if so, what type of development should be permitted. Change of use, however, can also have an impact on the environment and these laws have been used to stop or delay projects which are taking place on commercial property in well developed areas. For example, the New York Court of Appeals has approved application of these laws to Manhattan highrise apartments, reasoning that environmental impacts include virtually all quality of life issues including population density and changes in the ethnic make up of a community.

In most states, an environmental impact statement will be required for projects that are deemed to have potentially significant environmental impacts. The goal of these laws is to make sure that before projects are approved, a hard look is taken at the potential impacts. Because governmental approvals must be public and public interest groups have the right to participate in the process, the process is often long and costly. On controversial projects, public hearings are often held. Criticism of a draft environmental impact statement at public hearings often leads to revisions in the environmental impact statement or in the project which take time and are costly. Citizens groups have been quite effective in delaying or defeating projects both by suing government agencies to require them to take a closer look at the environmental impacts of a proposed project and by mobilizing public opposition that leads to a political decision not to approve the project.

In short, regardless of how simple the project appears to be, one should be prepared to need to hire experts and prove that it is, in fact, a simple project. Also, it is not uncommon for developers who anticipate difficulty to retain a public relations firm to assist them from the outset.

Hazardous Substances

Construction projects can be impacted by a wide variety of "hazardous substance" regulations. Asbestos may be the most prominent regulated substance that construction workers deal with. As we have already seen, EPA and other government agencies need to be notified in advance of certain asbestos projects, strict work practice requirements exist, and in many states, workers need special training and certifications or licenses. Indeed, renovation or demolition of a building that contains asbestos is often illegal without prior removal of the asbestos. Lead paint is another substance that is coming under very strict regulation. Many of the work practices now required for working with asbestos are being required for lead paint removal, and many cities now require removal of lead paint from residential buildings.

The number of regulated substances that construction workers may come into contact with is quite broad. From PCBs in lighting fixtures to formaldehyde, the number of substances about which questions are raised and regulations generated is growing. Indeed, OSHA has set permissible exposure limits for such common construction items as sawdust and welding fumes.

There are a variety of ways for regulated parties to become aware of what substances are regulated and how they are regulated. With regard to products purchased for use by employees, the manufacturer should include a material safety data sheet (MSDS) that details the dangers associated with the product and how to use the product safely. With regard to "in-place" building materials, one often needs to hire an environmental consultant to determine exactly what they will be working with. With asbestos, for example, some asbestos-containing products are easily recognizable while others appear to be nothing more than paint. It is wise to sample all suspect materials prior to working with them.

One of the central elements of OSHA's hazard communication standard, the written hazard communication program, requires employers to examine their worksites and the materials used. This process leads to greater awareness of potential hazards and easier compliance with the law.

Trade associations, through meetings, conferences and publications also serve a role of educating the regulated community. Often the trade association is merely publicizing enforcement activity, but enforcement activity within a regulated community is a great educator. It makes the rest of the community aware of the requirements as well as the fact that the regulators are actively involved. One should not, however, wait to learn what is required by being accused of a violation. By regular review of a limited number of publications, one can follow the regulatory process as it might effect them. Environmental counsel or an in-house regulatory affairs person could review the federal and state registers for proposed regulatory changes that may affect their industry. They should also review the publications that are devoted to that industry since such publications will almost always have information regarding changing regulations.

In addition to the regular review for new developments, many companies perform annual or semiannual compliance audits. These are merely an internal review of compliance procedures designed to assure that the information gathering process is translating itself into actions that are necessary both to prevent the costs related to enforcement actions and the damage to reputation such actions can cause.

Buried Substances

There was a time when if one was digging and struck oil they became rich. Now the opposite may be true. A construction crew that is digging a foundation and strikes a plume of some petroleum product or an underground tank, has a serious problem. The removal of abandoned underground storage tanks is strictly regulated and quite costly, and disposal of contaminated soil is also costly. Moreover, the amount of cleaning up (environmental remediation) one needs to do could be controlled by a state bureaucracy that adds further time and expense to the project.

Sick Buildings--Regulation of HVAC Systems

Sick buildings syndrome is the name given to a group of illnesses or symptoms experienced by building occupants. In certain buildings, large numbers of employees within the building complain of similar respiratory problems and those problems are attributed to the building in which they work. This is one of the chief problems related to indoor air quality. The issue of "indoor air quality" is becoming increasingly subject to regulation. The cause of sick buildings syndrome or poor indoor air quality is usually a problem with the heating, ventilation and air conditioning system. Thus, the regulation of indoor air usually means the regulation of the design and construction of such systems.

Interestingly, newer buildings, which are built for heating efficiency, often permit less fresh air in and, therefore, are more likely to have sick-buildings problems. Since redesign of a system can be quite costly, builders save a great deal of money by designing and constructing buildings with an eye toward better indoor air quality.

Other causes of indoor air problems include emissions of chemicals from wall board, furniture or carpeting and cigarettes. New carpeting in particular has been implicated in respiratory problems. As our ability to detect minute emissions of potentially harmful substances increases, the likelihood is that such emissions will become regulated.

STORING AND HANDLING OF CHEMICALS

Hazard Communication

OSHA's Hazard Communication Standard requires employers to maintain material safety data sheets for all hazardous chemicals in the workplace and to have a written hazard communication program that describes how information regarding these chemicals is to be made available to employees. Hazardous chemical is defined very broadly to include anything capable of causing injury.

Even cleaning supplies sold to the general public contain hazardous chemicals. With regard to cleaning supplies that contain hazardous chemicals, OSHA states that if employees are using consumer products with the same frequency and duration that consumers would ordinarily use them, then hazard communication does not apply. However, if the products are not ordinarily sold to consumers or are used by employees with greater frequency or duration than by consumers, hazard communication applies. There is a good chance, therefore, that OSHA hazard communication will apply to cleaning services and maintenance employees.

The determination of whether something is a hazardous chemical is to be made by manufacturers and importers and passed on to other employers. The manufacturer or importer of a hazardous chemical must sell it only with a material safety data sheet which has the information about risks and safe handling users will need. Therefore, an employer who is not a manufacturer or importer should not need to determine what hazardous chemicals are present in the workplace, other than by reviewing MSDS's and labels and perhaps writing to manufacturers.

Storage Tanks

Storage of hazardous chemicals or petroleum products in tanks is often a regulated activity. At the federal level, the Resource

Conservation and Recovery Act contains provisions related to underground storage tanks and the Clean Water Act contains spill prevention provisions. Additionally, many states and localities have regulations relating to tank design and registration.

Those who use or store large quantities of hazardous chemicals must also be aware of the reporting requirements imposed by the federal community right-to-know law ("EPCRA"). This law requires the reporting of storage and releases of listed hazardous chemicals to EPA and to state and local emergency planning agencies. EPCRA imposes only paperwork requirements, but the fines for noncompliance can be great.

Retailers

Retailers whose employees handle hazardous chemicals in sealed containers, but do not use the chemicals, do not need to have a written hazard communication program for such employees. They do need, however, to provide information and training to such employees because of the possibility of exposure if a container breaks. As with the cleaning supplies described above, Hazard Communication does not apply to consumer products which employees are exposed to in the same manner and with the same frequency as ordinary consumers.

OSHA also requires those who repackage or relabel chemicals to assure that accurate safety information is passed on to the subsequent purchasers. This will often mean merely that warnings that come in with a product go out with the product.

Retailers should also be cognizant of a trend toward localized regulation of chemicals. For example, California's Proposition 65 requires warnings by businesses that expose people to carcinogens. This has placed a burden both on retailers and on manufacturers who need to package certain goods specifically to satisfy this rule.

Warehouses

Warehouses will be subject to virtually the same hazard communication rules as retailers. They may also have responsibilities pursuant to EPCRA.

EPCRA requires businesses that use or store hazardous chemicals to provide emergency response information to EPA and state or local emergency planning agencies. Among the substances about which one is required to provide information are all hazardous chemicals for which one must maintain an MSDS pursuant to OSHA's Hazard Communication Standard. Because of quantity limitations in the community right-to-know law, warehouses are more likely than retail outlets to have responsibilities under this law.

It is interesting to note that EPCRA was largely a response to the incident in Bhopal, India in which a leak from a chemical plant caused many deaths. The law, however, is much broader and requires reporting regarding numerous chemicals, the storage of which provides little or no risk to the local community.

Manufacturing

As with other businesses, what environmental regulations apply to a given manufacturing process will greatly depend on what substances are being used. As previously discussed, it is usually not difficult to determine whether a given substance is regulated by EPA, OSHA or a state or local agency. The more difficult issues for manufacturers are determining whether their wastes are hazardous and determining whether the products they produce may be hazardous. Because there are relatively few substances that have been thoroughly studied and even fewer combinations of substances whose effects have been studied, RCRA and the Clean Water Act both provide "characteristics" tests to determine whether something should be treated as toxic or hazardous. With regard to the Clean Water Act, the pollution control technology, the effluent limits and the testing procedures will all be part of the discharge permit. One will ordinarily be prohibited from discharging waste without such a permit. Thus, testing of effluent will probably take place during permit negotiations and on a regular schedule thereafter.

The RCRA characteristics test will be relevant only if one generates solid waste that may be hazardous. Unlike the Clean Water Act which permits discharge pursuant to a permit, RCRA requires that if one generates waste that is considered to be hazardous, the generator must package the waste properly and, by a manifest system, establish that it has been sent to a permitted facility via a permitted carrier.

OSHA hazard communication requires manufacturers to determine whether their product is hazardous and if so, to prepare a material safety data sheet to accompany each sale. This can be a very difficult task. It requires a great deal of scientific expertise to devise testing procedures and perform the testing. The legal issues related to when an MSDS (or a product warning) is required are unclear enough that legal advice may be necessary. Manufacturers are likely to already be familiar with a similar set of decisions that needs to be made regarding warnings for product liability purposes. While the MSDS requirement and the product liability warning requirement are not identical, many of the same factors go into the decision-making process.

Environmental Marketing

Public awareness of environmental issues has caused a great deal of marketing or advertising based on environmental claims. Claims that a particular chemical or compound is not used in the product have been made for a long time and are easy to verify. Claims that something is recyclable or biodegradable on the other hand, are virtually impossible to test because the meaning of these terms is not firmly established. For example, is something recyclable when no one yet recycles it. One could argue that recyclable means the product has some potential to be recycled. Is something biodegradable when studies indicate that under common landfill conditions it will not break down in several hundred years. Again, the argument can be made that the term refers to the capability of biodegrading, not whether it will quickly biodegrade under ordinary conditions. Is something made of recycled material when more than 90% of the material used in making the product is not recycled? It clearly contains some recycled material.

While claims that a product is recyclable or biodegradable are both hard to prove and hard to disprove, the emotions surrounding such issues make it likely that false advertising or "environmental fraud" actions will be brought by public interest groups, if not by the government. Environmental public interest groups closely monitor environmental claims and have the means to police accuracy by publicity or litigation, (even if they are merely policing their own version of accuracy). Businesses that are not careful about their environmental claims are thus likely to find that such claims increase sales in the short term but create a public relations nightmare in the long term. One would be best advised to use caution.

A number of organizations have recommended definitions of the relevant terminology that they hope will be uniformly adopted so that we can all mean the same thing when we say the same thing. While the processes by which these organizations work are less open than agency rulemaking procedures, regulated parties have several interests in providing input during the drafting process. First, when the regulators begin drafting, they often pay a great deal of attention to what they view as industry standards. To the extent that these organizations are attempting to create such standards, regulators are likely to pay a great deal of attention. Second, the standards regarding what is feasible in the recycling area can vary from industry to industry. The organizations will therefore need the input from members of each industry so that the standards they set make sense in the real world.

New York State has issued regulations regarding recycling emblems and use of terms such as recycled and recyclable. In defining recycled, the state responds to the two most prevalent abuses relating to use of that term: (1) some people use the phrase made from recycled material when only a very small percentage of the material is recycled; and (2) some make the claim when none of the material was ever part of a product that was sold prior to recycling. In response, the regulations distinguish between post-consumer material material that has been sold, has served its intended use and is ready to be discarded and secondary material, which includes both post-consumer material and certain pre-consumer materials such as waste from the manufacturing process. The regulations also specify minimum amounts of both post-consumer and secondary material that are required before a product can be considered to be "recycled." These minimum amounts vary greatly from product to product.

In defining recyclable, the regulations focus on whether the product or material is currently being recycled in the location in which the claim is being made. The term recyclable may only be used for things actually recycled in that locality.

Questions can be raised about whether and to what extent the New York regulations regulate the marketing of items outside of New York that are also sold in New York and, by ripple effect, the behavior of many outside of New York. There is likely to be litigation regarding the scope and effect of the New York regulations, particularly as they affect both speech and interstate commerce. There is little question, however, that in the area of marketing and use of language, national uniformity is essential. It therefore makes sense for marketers outside of New York to examine these regulations and begin to answer questions such as, can I live with this? and, if not, what can I do to see that this does not happen here?, or if it does happen here, what can I do to make sure it doesn't happen in exactly the same way?.

CHAPTER VIII

EFFECTS OF THE ENVIRONMENTAL REGULATORY PROCESS ON CONTRACTS

This chapter will discuss how the environmental regulatory process may have an impact on the meaning of contracts to which you may presently be a party and conversely, how that process could affect on the contracts you may enter into. Among the key topics covered in this chapter will be how the Superfund Law has changed the meaning of many of the terms in the standard comprehensive general liability insurance policy, how changes in environmental regulations impact on risks that may have been allocated in prior agreements and how you can structure your future agreements to take some of these changes into account.

The first question you are likely to raise about the above is that contracts are agreements between private individuals; therefore how can the government, by regulation or otherwise, change those agreements? The question is a good one and has some basis in the Constitution which prohibits the government from impairing the validity of existing contracts. Here, however, what the government has done through regulation is to raise questions about the relationship of the parties that are either not dealt with in the contract or not adequately dealt with. Thus, rather than changing the contract, these changes in the regulations affect the questions raised about the contract and sometimes lead to answers that were unforseen at the time of contracting.

The superfund law has caused major changes in the insurance industry as well as in the meaning of insurance contracts. An insurance contract is just like any other contract in that it is made to embody an agreement. You agree to pay premiums and they agree to pay you certain amounts if specified events occur. Thus, when there is litigation regarding an insurance contract and the question of "was there a contract" arises, the court looks for evidence that there were terms upon which the parties agreed. In interpreting an insurance contract, as with other contracts, the general rule is that the intent of the parties controls. Insurance agreements tend to be less of a negotiated agreement than most contracts. That is, often, the insurance company drafts the policy (the agreement) and presents it to the insured who signs it. The insured thus often does not participate actively in the drafting, and may therefore have no specific intent at the time of contracting and no awareness of the meaning of the agreement. This can put the insured at a disadvantage when the issue of the meaning of the agreement arises both because things he may have expected may not be in the agreement and because he will have few credible arguments regarding what he reasonably expected or how he understood language in the agreement.

Some courts recognize that insurance agreements are often presented to the insured and not negotiated, and protect persons who sign unaware by applying a rule that interprets ambiguity in the agreement against the drafter (i.e. against the insurance company). Nevertheless, sophisticated business people who negotiate many other agreements can better protect themselves by reading, questioning and negotiating to assure that what they are signing satisfies their needs.

The standard Comprehensive General Liability (CGL) policy issued in the 1950's and 1960's said nothing about pollution. It said that if an accident results in unintended or unexpected injury within the policy period, the insurer will defend all suits and indemnify the insured for damages. The Superfund Law gives the government the power to require the cleanup of hazardous waste sites. It permits the government to order potentially responsible persons, including persons who owned property on which hazardous substances were deposited and persons who delivered hazardous waste to a site, regardless of how long ago, to remediate the site. Whether the old CGL policies (e.g. from the 1950's and 1960's) provide the insured with coverage in such a case depends on such questions as (1) is an order by an administrative agency (EPA) a lawsuit for which the contract provides defense or indemnity? (2) was the dumping or delivery of the waste an accident? (3) was the damage that results from the dumping unexpected? (4) are remediation costs covered "damages"? and (5) which insurer is responsible, the one at the time of dumping or the one at the time of cleanup? A vast amount of litigation has taken place and is taking place regarding the application of these old insurance policies to superfund cleanup actions. The results of this litigation have often seen courts interpreting the policies to provide coverage for claims not in anyone's contemplation at the time of contract.

The standard CGL policy was changed in the early 1970's to add a pollution exclusion. This clause provides, basically, that no coverage is provided for pollution unless the pollution is "sudden and accidental." The meaning of that clause has been the subject of a great deal of debate and litigation and court decisions have varied widely. Since some courts have held that intentional dumping of a hazardous chemical for a long period of time can result in property damage that is "sudden and accidental," there is virtually no cleanup action in which insurance issues cannot be raised.

Some insurance companies now include a so-called absolute pollution exclusion, which purports to exclude all pollution claims. This exclusion has provided better protection for insurers. Insureds thus need to know what clause is in their present policies as well as their past policies to better understand their rights and how changes in environmental law may effect these rights.

The trigger of coverage issue has also had a major impact on the insurance industry. By trigger of coverage, courts mean what event during the policy period causes there to be coverage under the policy. The policies usually require "injury" during the policy period, but in the environmental context it is often difficult to determine when injury first occurs. Some courts have read the injury requirement to mean that all policies from the first exposure to hazardous substances are "triggered" because some injury must have occurred during all of them. Thus, old policies that everyone thought had long expired may now be of great value and the same injury may trigger numerous policies. One result of this has been the growing use of the "claims made" policy, a policy which provides coverage only for claims made during the policy period. This policy permits insurance companies to protect themselves from the need to cover potential latent injuries. Such policies, however, often provide little coverage. The alternative is for insureds to insist on occurrence-based coverage, which covers occurrences during the policy period regardless of when they are asserted.

Leases

Changes in environmental law have also had an impact on the meaning of fairly standard lease terms. For example, the tenant commonly agrees to assure compliance with all applicable laws, regulations, court orders, etc. A tenant who receives a PRP letter from EPA may be responsible for cleanup of hazardous waste on the site as operator of the facility. If the tenant goes to the landlord, the landlord may say you (tenant) have agreed to be responsible for this. The PRP letter is, after all, a regulation or court order. Tenant's reply may be that it didn't do the dumping, a prior tenant did. Therefore, the landlord should pay for cleanup. More importantly, the cleanup will benefit the landlord more than the tenant. Landlord's response to this may be that the superfund law doesn't really care who did the dumping or who will benefit; tenant is responsible both as present operator of the facility and by the lease agreement.

Such issues were probably not considered at the time the lease was entered into and are therefore not adequately dealt with in standard form leases. Negotiating a resolution to these issues is often difficult and if there is litigation, it will be costly and the results will be difficult to predict. Such problems demonstrate the need for foresight in drafting new leases to avoid these problems in the future.

Changing the above scenario slightly, assume that the lease said that tenant takes the premises "as is" and asbestos containing materials in the premises have deteriorated to the state that (a) no renovation of the tenant space can be performed without the expense of removing the asbestos and (b) even without a planned renovation, removal may be the most prudent means to avoid future costs and liabilities. Tenant goes to the landlord and says--you put the asbestos there, you should remove it. Landlord says, you took the premises as is and there is no law requiring removal. While the outcome of the negotiation may depend on such factors as whether the tenant wants to do renovations and the length of the tenancy, if litigation results, the outcome will be difficult to predict.

In both of the above cases, the changing regulatory scheme has created risks that were not thought of and therefore not allocated in existing agreements. The results are very difficult negotiations which often lead to costly litigation and a strong case for careful structuring of future agreements.

Asbestos may be an easy case when discussing future costs because one can fairly easily determine the amount and condition of the asbestos-containing materials and estimate the likelihood of the need for response actions and the cost of the likely responses. A landlord that does not want to pay for removal can forbid the tenant from taking any action that may impact on the asbestos and require that the tenant pay for asbestos-related costs if it does take such actions. A tenant who does not want to pay for asbestos removal can look for another building or use the asbestos NESHAPS as a bargaining tool. The NESHAPS require asbestos removal before demolition and before certain renovation projects. An owner cannot contract away NESHAP responsibilities. Thus, the landlord will have to remove the asbestos sometime (before demolition) and if the tenant removes it without following the NESHAPS, the landlord may have liability.

Other hazardous substances are likely to be less predictable and there is therefore greater uncertainty as to what potential costs need to be allocated. That uncertainty should not prevent well thought out drafting and negotiation. Indeed, often agreements go so far as to allocate the risk that the law will change rendering some of today's permissible activities illegal.

Indemnities

It is not unusual for contracts, whether they are purchase and sale agreements or service agreements, to contain an indemnity clause. Commonly, one party will agree to indemnify (reimburse) the other for all costs incurred as a result of claims caused by the negligent act of the one giving the indemnity. In its simplest case, A as contractor agrees to indemnify B, as building owner for claims against B that are caused by A's negligence. Thus, if A negligently builds a building for B and the building falls on top of C, when C sues B, the indemnity agreement requires A to pay B all costs related to the suit. Usually, the active party gives the indemnity. However, where both parties are required by the agreement to take certain actions, cross-indemnities may be appropriate. In a cross-indemnity, both parties agree to indemnify the other for injuries they cause.

Such standard indemnities may not be helpful in the superfund context because superfund does not require negligence (it is a strict liability statute) and does not require that a PRP be a cause of the damage. All it requires is disposal of or release of a hazardous substance. Thus, if A sells property to B and agrees to indemnify B for all claims arising out of injuries caused by A's negligence, claims arising out of the presence of hazardous substances may not be covered. The purchaser clearly wants to be protected from those, but the seller may not have caused them and even if seller caused them, he may not have been negligent.

If a buyer, builder, lessee, etc. wants protection from the results of the presence or release of hazardous substances, it needs to structure the agreement so that intent is clear. Standard indemnity language is not likely to do it.

The environmental regulatory process, thus has had a major impact on both how past agreements are read and how future issues need to be assessed in structuring future agreements.

CHAPTER IX

ENVIRONMENTAL PROFESSIONALS

Most environmental problems that a business faces are solved with a combination of legal expertise and scientific expertise. For example, to negotiate permit conditions, environmental counsel will know the legal requirements and the extent of the powers of the agency, while an environmental consultant will be needed for issues such as how to comply and what effluent limits are feasible. To engage in due diligence for a transaction, counsel will be helpful in determining what documents and conditions to examine, an environmental consultant will be needed to examine the conditions and, if necessary, sample environmental media. This chapter will discuss putting the team together.

Environmental Consultants

The first thing to remember when engaging an environmental consultant is that not all environmental consultants have the same expertise. Some are engineers. Some are industrial hygienists. And some have degrees in environmental science.

Even among those with the same expertise, their experience may differ greatly. Some do mostly groundwater investigation and remediation. Some do more transactional due diligence. Some do more work with regard to permitting. Some are primarily Superfund remediation contractors. One needs to know what they are looking for and examine the credentials of the consultant carefully.

Most environmental consultants will have some sort of brochure or advertising material that sets forth their qualifications and describes some of the larger projects they have been involved in. This will give a good idea of the scope of the consultant's expertise and the area of emphasis. Some consulting firms are very specialized. Others are very large and capable of handling a large number of different types of projects. Most consultants will be willing to provide references and, time permitting, one can learn a good deal by checking references.

Many businesses have their environmental counsel retain the environmental consultant. Environmental counsel will often have experience with a variety of consultants and be in a position to make recommendations with regard to who is good for what issues. Environmental counsel also has the background and experience to ask the types of questions that will provide a better evaluation of potential candidates.

In many cases, one will need proof of qualification as well as proof of appropriate experience. For example, RCRA (the Resource Conservation and Recovery Act) regulations require a certified professional engineer to certify closure of certain treatment storage and disposal facilities. Again, environmental counsel should be in a position to provide advice regarding what qualifications, licenses or certifications the consultant should have.

Retaining the Consultant

Environmental consultants are often retained by counsel. Among the primary reasons for this is the creation or preservation of any evidentiary privilege that may be available. Of course, the strength of this reason will vary with the context. Thus, if the consultant is engaged to provide support for pending or potential litigation, the need for confidentiality is usually greater than when the consultant is retained in the transactional context. Many will have the consultant retained by counsel regardless of the context both to protect whatever confidentiality may be available and to make it easier for the attorney to use the consultant as a means of providing sound legal advice.

Other business people prefer to retain the consultant directly. Some do so because, as managers, they like to be able to manage all aspects of the project (the legal and the scientific). Others see that as a means of better controlling costs.

Regardless of whether the consultant is to be retained directly or through counsel, counsel should be involved in preparing or reviewing the agreement with the consultant. Since legal or regulatory considerations are often a driving force in the need for an environmental consultant, counsel should also play a role in creating the description of the services to be performed or the scope of the work.

Along with the scope of the work, other terms that are often negotiated are the scope of the consultant's responsibility, insurance requirements, the type of report the client wants (written, oral, with or without recommendations), time of performance, and confidentiality.

Environmental Counsel

A general practitioner is an attorney whose practice includes matters in a variety of legal fields. Many attorneys, on the other hand, practice primarily in one field and consider themselves to be an environmental lawyer, a corporate lawyer, a real estate lawyer, etc. There are no separate bar exams for these different types of lawyers. Thus, calling oneself an environmental lawyer does not indicate that one has any certificate, or degree in environmental law. It merely implies that one's practice emphasizes environmental issues. There are a number of advantages to specialization. In particular, one can find answers more quickly and should have a greater awareness of the subtle practicalities in an area of the law he or she deals with regularly.

As the field of environmental law has grown, it has become very difficult for an attorney to be knowledgeable about all aspects of environmental law. Broadly, there are those who specialize in or whose practice emphasizes environmental litigation, those who are primarily transactional (they provide advice or documentation for real estate or corporate transactions) and those who are primarily involved in providing compliance assistance or advice. Thus, one can be an environmental lawyer and have a great deal of environmental experience and yet have no knowledge about or experience in dealing with the environmental issue you need to have resolved.

Within the group of environmental litigators, there are those who do nothing but superfund work, those who specialize in litigation regarding environmental review statutes and those who have environmental litigation as a subspeciality of some other field such as real estate litigation, corporate litigation or white collar criminal defense.

There are transactional (real estate and corporate) attorneys who have some knowledge and expertise in environmental matters, transactional attorneys who are at firms that have an environmental group to assist with the environmental aspects of a transaction, and transactional lawyers who farm out the environmental aspects of a transaction to specialists.

Among the compliance attorneys, there are those who are, broadly speaking, regulatory advisors, who provide advice regarding a variety of statutes and regulatory agencies, those who have expertise on specific pieces of legislation or the regulatory scheme related to a particular issue (e.g., an expert on asbestos regulations), and those who specialize in assisting clients in obtaining permits.

The above groupings are not nearly as well-defined as the above discussion may imply. Many matters start out as regulatory compliance and end up as litigation. Permit matters are part transactional and contain regulatory advice and negotiation with the regulators.

Additionally, it is not unusual for a permitting procedure to have litigated aspects to it. People are likely to have areas of emphasis, but it will be rare for anyone to do just one thing. It would, thus, be rare for a client to switch attorneys each time a new lawyering skill is required.

It is also important when looking at the class of people who consider themselves to be environmental attorneys to remember that the environment is often a political or emotional issue. Many environmental attorneys, therefore, have their own agenda in mind, or start working on a matter with some preconceived idea of right and wrong. Since it is virtually impossible to be an effective advocate for a position one does not believe in, it is important to get a sense of what the personal beliefs (or biases) of an environmental attorney or firm are before you retain them. It is also helpful to discuss prior experience with an attorney before making a decision to retain him or her. Does the attorney's prior experience in the area say anything about how your case will be handled? Does the prior experience indicate an aggressive nature? Does prior experience fighting projects similar to the one you are defending raise questions about the attorney's beliefs or does it give the attorney an advantage because he or she knows what the other side will argue? While the answers to these questions will have different meaning to different clients, they are the sort of questions one needs to explore to assure the right match.

When Do You Need Counsel?

Every attorney has a group of stories designed to make the point that if only this client had contacted me before they acted, they could have saved themselves a great deal of money or made a project much simpler. Many members of the regulated community can probably also tell stories of attorneys they fired for creating work for themselves or milking a project. There is probably truth on both sides of this fence.

In discussing when to consult with counsel, we will start with the easiest case and work backwards to the harder cases. When a claim is asserted against you by a regulatory agency, you should have counsel review the claim quickly. The time to respond to the claim will vary both with the agency and the forum. OSHA, for example, gives a regulated party roughly two weeks to object to a proposed penalty and the failure to respond in that quick time frame could be a waiver of any defenses you may have.

Since the costs of noncompliance, including defense of an enforcement action and penalties, are often greater than the costs of compliance, it makes sense to consult with counsel regarding compliance at some point prior to the alleged violation. At a minimum, a prudent business person will want to assess the costs of compliance and the risks (potential costs) associated with noncompliance and make an informed decision. Legal counsel is usually best suited to assess those risks, but portions of that assessment may also require scientific expertise.

Environmental counsel should be able to provide advice regarding minimally what must be done to comply as well as, practically, what are some of the means of compliance that satisfy the agency in a cost effective manner. Additionally, counsel should have a sense of what issues the agency is currently most concerned about. While that does not necessarily mean that other problems will not be found or prosecuted, it can give one sense of what problems are most likely to be discovered and what problems are most likely to be treated seriously by the agency. This information can be quite helpful in the decision making process.

Often, to determine the most efficient or effective compliance methods, counsel will need the assistance of an environmental consultant. There is some confusion in the regulated community regarding the division of labor between an environmental consulting firm and environmental attorneys. That confusion is caused in large part by attempts by both sets of professionals to claim expertise in the other's area of expertise. More specifically, consultants often give advice on the regulations and attorneys often give practical health and safety advice. In many cases, the assistance of both experts is necessary, and prudent use of both means limiting the scope of their tasks to their appropriate area of expertise.

The National Environmental Policy Act requires federal government agencies to examine all projects and activities which they will be performing or supporting and consider the environmental impacts of those projects and activities. The act is procedural, it requires a review, but does not require avoidance of particular impacts. Regulated parties are well-advised to engage in a similar procedure. That is, before engaging in a new activity and finding yourself in a regulatory morass, a brief examination of the potential environmental and regulatory problems can save a great deal of time and aggravation. An examination of the environmental health and safety regulatory problems may differ from examination of potential environmental problems because there are environmental regulations which are not necessarily related to any environmental health or safety issue. Unfortunately, not all actions which are environmentally sound are free from environmental regulatory problems. That is a primary reason why an environmental consultant's view of what acts are environmentally sound will not assure regulatory compliance.

Additionally, because environmental regulations are changing rapidly (at least when compared with other areas of the law), one needs to make an effort to stay abreast of changes, both to avoid unpleasant surprises and to attempt to impact on proposals that could affect your business. Trade associations often keep their members abreast of proposed changes. Environmental attorneys often do the same. Such a procedure permits the client to react quickly to changes and to consider, on a case-by-case basis, the need or desirability to having counsel involved.

Finally, we need to note that when to have environmental counsel involved depends a lot on the individual regulated party. Some are so cautious that they want the advice of counsel before every step. Others only want counsel to bail them out of emergencies. The wiser course is a case-by-case approach in which the activity, the regulatory scheme, and the potential liabilities are weighed to determine whether and when to get counsel involved.

CHAPTER X

SOURCES OF FURTHER INFORMATION
ENVIRONMENTAL LAW

In legal research, sources are generally divided into two broad categories--primary sources and secondary sources. Primary sources are the law itself, while secondary sources discuss and interpret the law. The primary sources are the statutes, regulations and court decisions. Virtually everything else is secondary. An attorney is wise to refer to primary sources whenever possible and secondary sources for answers to questions not found in any primary source. The regulated community, however, will often not have the patience to wade through the mass of information that can be produced by Congress or EPA. It is also not likely to possess the familiarity with the primary sources needed to find one's way quickly. Secondary sources will probably, therefore, be more useful for them. A middle ground exists in books that combine the two. That is, some publications provide the primary sources on a given issue and some discussion of or a guide to using those primary sources.

Among the secondary sources one should distinguish between those intended to provide practical advice and those that are more academic in nature. Practitioners often write about their area of practice, explaining what the rules are and how they are applied. No self-respecting academic would devote a great deal of time to explaining what the rules are. They prefer to focus on why the rules are what they are and what the rules ought to be.

An attorney has a need for both sets of secondary sources. The more practical sources will have quick answers to every day questions, while the academic sources will have ideas that can be used to create arguments in difficult or novel situations. To the layman, however, academic sources are likely to be fascinating but relatively useless.

Primary Sources

The primary sources can be found in a variety of formats from official reporters to loose leaf services and computer data bases. In most cases, the best source from an attorney's point of view will not necessarily be the best source from the point of view of the regulated party. With statutes, for example, the United States Code Annotated has more than 200 volumes and covers a much more diverse set of issues than any regulated party could be interested in. Each state has an official "Annotated" Code which includes numerous volumes and covers every area of law for which there is a statute. By annotated, they mean that after each section of law they include a list of cases that have discussed or interpreted that section. This is an important research tool for lawyers, but a regulated party seldom wants to go to half a dozen case books to see what the law means.

For federal cases, the official reporters are the Federal Supplement for trial court decisions, Federal Reporter for appellate decisions and United States Reports for Supreme Court decisions. Each state will also have its own official reporter or reporters. The order in which official reporters print cases has nothing to do with subject matter. The cases found in reporters cover a greater number of subjects than the annotated codes. Thus, if one is looking for information on a particular area of the law, official reporters are not the most handy reference. Additionally, because court decisions are rendered daily on a wide variety of subjects, official reporters will take up a great deal of space in one's library. The Federal Reporter Second Series, for example, has now gone beyond its 900th volume.

It is also important to note that cases, even when collected and organized by subject are often not the easiest reference. A court decision usually contains a discussion on a number of different issues, so that someone interested in a particular subject often needs to leaf through a great deal of irrelevant material before getting to the answer to the question at hand. Additionally, judges seldom give yes or no answers. A court decision is often a piece of advocacy in which a judge gives a detailed description of the background of the law and then a discussion of all the reasons for the decision. Reading cases is a skill, the development of which takes virtually the whole first year of law school. Thus one looking for easy access to practical advice on what the law is, will seldom want to read many cases.

The Code of Federal Regulations ("CFR"), the official repository of federal regulations, is also not the handiest of tools. As with the above sources, the number of volumes, diversity of materials and lack of guidance material makes it not the best source for easy answers.

The Federal Register, as the first place in which regulations appear, can be a fairly handy source. For some time after the appearance of a regulation in the Federal Register, there is likely to be no other source. Additionally, the Federal Register notice almost always contains a detailed preamble, which is the agency's explanation of the reasons for the regulations and the meaning of the regulations. This preamble is an important secondary source, but it is very close to being a primary source. That means that while the preamble is not, strictly speaking, the law, it is quite authoritative.

A number of publishers publish sets of cases organized by topics. For example, the Environmental Law Reporter, collects and publishes cases relating to environmental law. These services provide a good method for staying aware of what the latest cases in a given area are. They publish, however, in more or less chronological order, not by subject within the broad topic of environmental law. Additionally, they publish the entire case, not just an excerpt relevant to environmental law. Thus, while these collections are much easier to use than the official reporter, they are not likely to be sufficiently handy for use by nonlawyers.

Mixed Primary and Secondary Sources

It is difficult to describe the mixed sources without describing the "systems" developed by certain legal publishers, because each publisher takes the primary sources and adds to or organizes them to a different degree.

West Publishing Company is probably the largest legal publishing company. It publishes regional reporters that contain the reported cases of all the states, annotated codes for federal laws and for many of the states, and a wide variety of materials designed for law students. West is probably best known for its key number digest system. West has divided the law into subjects like an outline of the law and assigned numbers to each subject. Its digest system is a set of volumes organized by subject with a listing of all the cases on that subject. West's digests have become an invaluable research tool for law students and attorneys. When West publishes a case (in its unofficial reporters), it divides the case into sections, assigning a key number from its digest system to each section of the case. West's digests of the law, or the Westlaw computerized database can then be used to find other cases on similar subjects merely by using the key number. The West key number system is a great finding tool for lawyers, but it is a tool for finding cases, not for finding quick answers. It is therefore, not something we highly recommend for nonlawyers.

A number of publishers, including Government Institutes, publish collections of environmental statutes and/or regulations. These are often one-volume collections and can be a very handy reference.

Looseleaf reporters are precisely that, looseleaf binders for which subscribers receive weekly inserts, so they can stay up-to-date regarding changes in the law. For example, the Bureau of National

Affairs publishes a looseleaf set called the Environment Reporter. The set contains federal and state environmental laws and regulations, EPA Policy Statements, environmental cases and weekly summaries of new laws or key cases. The set is well indexed so that answers to questions can be fairly easily accessed. With the weekly inserts one receives detailed directions as to where to add pages and where pages are being replaced. It is thus a useful combination of primary and secondary sources or a collection of portions of primary sources, organized and indexed to facilitate easy use.

Environment Law Handbooks

Government Institutes publishes an environmental law series that combines primary and secondary sources with the primary goal of providing easy access to clear concise answers. Government Institutes publishes some 35 subject-related handbooks (e.g., "Environmental Law Handbook," "Above Ground Storage Tank Management" etc.). Each is written by experienced professionals.

These books provide a clear description of relevant rules and procedures and usually include an appendix that contains key provisions of the statutes and regulations. While the West System uses the primary sources to help find other primary sources, the Government Institutes volumes are primarily a secondary source, with the primary sources attached for easy reference. Thus, in contrast to the West System, which is designed to help you find other sources, Government Institutes books are designed to provide self-contained, practical advice.

Government Institutes also publishes state environmental law handbooks. These are written by law firms in each state and designed to relate specifically to the rules of that state. Both the federal and state handbooks are often used as course texts for courses conducted by Government Institutes at which the authors serve as speakers.

Secondary Sources

Secondary sources include law reviews, treatises and anything written about the law that is not the law itself. Because the purpose of these varies so greatly, it is difficult to generalize. Law reviews are usually scholarly in nature and often contain voluminous footnotes (citations to the primary sources). Magazines that report on particular issues will often have a legal affairs section which will try to provide practical advice. There are so many sources of information about environmental law that when the Practicing Law Institute put together materials entitled "Managing The Private Law Library" in 1989, the chapter on environmental law research listed more than 20 pages of what the author considered to be the "major" sources.

Choosing Among Secondary Sources

With such a wealth of materials available, one who plans to build a small reference library needs a method of choosing. One way to build a useful set is to find a publisher whose works satisfy a given need and stick with that publisher. At a minimum, that method will minimize the overlap between the volumes selected and prevent conflicts between the works relied upon. Certain legal publishers are known to carefully screen their authors and use attorneys in-house to further screen what those authors are saying. This process tends to produce a more reliable product. Publishers such as Government Institutes, that produce a number of related materials, have a thorough awareness of the needs of their readers and when selecting new topics are careful to avoid duplication or repetition while trying to fill gaps that may exist.

Another method of choosing among publications is by author. Sometimes, one can leaf through a number of secondary sources on a given subject and see that some of the authors are citing the work of another author. That author may be the one whose work you want to read. If he or she is relied upon by other authors, you should feel more comfortable relying on him or her. More importantly, a secondary source that relies heavily on other secondary sources is potentially unreliable. If you are going to rely on someone else's reading of the law, the one being relied upon ought at least to have read the law.

Another method of putting together a set on environmental law is to consult an environmental attorney. Talk about what you are interested in finding and get a sense of what he or she recommends. Talk about it, don't just buy what your environmental counsel has on his or her desk. There are several reasons for this. First, your needs may differ, so that what he or she uses might not be very useful to you. Second, and perhaps more important, attorneys often put together a larger collection and have several sources on the same subject. Some of the volumes in my office are used on an almost daily basis, others are, in my view, almost 95% drivel. In some cases, the purchase served a particular purpose and is now no longer useful. In some cases that other 5% is very valuable. And in some cases, the purchase was a mistake. One sitting in my office is not likely to be able to tell which is which. Therefore, someone carefully selecting their sources will not rely solely on the fact that someone else whose opinion they respect has purchased it. They will take the additional step of finding out why they purchased it and what it is good for.

Breadth of circulation is an attractive but somewhat misleading guide to what sources are useful or authoritative. You might think that the fact that many are purchasing a particular work, gives it some credibility. Often, however, that just means that many people have made the same mistake. There may be times when making the same mistake as others provides some comfort. In environmental compliance, however, it does not.

In sum, putting together a small useful library of secondary sources on environmental law can be difficult, but there are a number of shortcuts that can provide a good useful set.

Government Sources of Information

One final source of information on environmental law which should not be overlooked is the government. In addition to issuing regulations, EPA, OSHA and other government agencies publish a variety of materials that can provide helpful information. Most useful of those materials are guidance documents. In these, the agency attempts to provide compliance assistance or to provide advice concerning how to act in areas which may not yet be regulated. These are merely advisory. They are not the law. Nevertheless, there is some safety in following EPA's advice when the regulatory requirements are unclear. Other helpful government documents are internal materials discussing enforcement of the regulations. These can sometimes be obtained by a phone request or by a Freedom of Information request. Other times, the agency makes an enforcement directive public as a means of providing additional guidance to the regulated community. Government Institutes publishes a variety of these materials, most notably the EPA and OSHA inspection manuals. These are also not the law, but again provide information that can be very useful in making compliance decisions.

INDEX

About Government Institutes

Government Institutes, Inc. was founded in 1973 to provide continuing education and practical information for your professional development. Specializing in environmental, health and safety concerns, we recognize that you face unique challenges presented by the ever-increasing number of new laws and regulations and the rapid evolution of new technologies, methods and markets.

Our information and continuing education efforts include a Videotape Distribution Service, over 140 courses held nation-wide throughout the year, and over 150 publications, making us the world's largest publisher in these areas.

Government Institutes, Inc.
4 Research Place, Suite 200
Rockville, MD 20850
(301) 921-2300

Other related books published by Government Institutes:

Environmental Law Handbook, 12th Edition - The recognized authority in the field, this invaluable text, written by nationally-recognized legal experts, provides practical and current information on all major environmental areas. Hardcover/670 pages/Apr '93/$68 ISBN: 0-86587-350-X

Environmental Statutes, 1993 Edition - All the major environmental laws incorporated into one convenient source.
Hardcover/1,170 pages/Mar '93/$59   ISBN: 0-86587-352-6
Softcover/1,170 pages/Mar '93/$49   ISBN: 0-86587-351-8

Environmental Regulatory Glossary, 6th Edition - This glossary records and standardizes more than 4,000 terms, abbreviations and acronyms, all compiled directly from the environmental statutes or the U.S. Code of Federal Regulations. Hardcover/544 pages/May '93 $65   ISBN: 0-86587-353-4

Directory of Environmental Information Sources, 4th Edition - Details hard-to-find Federal Government Resources; State Government Resources; Professional, Scientific, and Trade Organizations; Newsletters, Magazines, and Periodicals; and Databases.
Softcover/350 pages/Nov '92/$74   ISBN: 0-86587-326-7

Environmental Audits, 6th Edition - Details how to begin and manage a successful audit program for your facility. Use these checklists and sample procedures to identify your problem areas. Softcover/ 592 pages/Nov '89/$75   ISBN: 0-86587-776-9

The Greening of American Business: Making Bottom-Line Sense of Environmental Responsibility - Written by leading environmental professionals from industry, law firms, and universities, this book explains how companies are coping with increasing demands that they engage in environmentally-sound business practices. Softcover 350 pages/Oct '92/$24.95 ISBN: 0-86587-295-3

Call the above number for our current book/video catalog and course schedule.